ISBN 978-1-333-71600-4
PIBN 10538613

1 MONTH OF
FREE
READING

at

www.ForgottenBooks.com

By purchasing this book you are
eligible for one month membership to
ForgottenBooks.com, giving you
unlimited access to our entire
collection of over 700,000 titles via
our web site and mobile apps.

To claim your free month visit:

www.forgottenbooks.com/free538613

English
Français
Deutsche
Italiano
Español
Português

www.forgottenbooks.com

Mythology Photography **Fiction**
Fishing Christianity **Art** Cooking
Essays Buddhism Freemasonry
Medicine **Biology** Music **Ancient
Egypt** Evolution Carpentry Physics
Dance Geology **Mathematics** Fitness
Shakespeare **Folklore** Yoga Marketing
Confidence Immortality Biographies
Poetry **Psychology** Witchcraft
Electronics Chemistry History **Law**
Accounting **Philosophy** Anthropology
Alchemy Drama Quantum Mechanics
Atheism Sexual Health **Ancient History**
Entrepreneurship Languages Sport
Paleontology Needlework Islam
Metaphysics Investment Archaeology
Parenting Statistics Criminology
Motivational

WOODWARD'S REMINISCENCES

OF THE

Creek, or Muscogee Indians,

Contained in Letters to Friends in

GEORGIA AND ALABAMA.

———— • —◆—• ————

BY THOMAS S. WOODWARD, OF LOUISIANA,
(FORMERLY OF ALABAMA.)

———— • —◆—• ————

WITH AN APPENDIX,
CONTAINING INTERESTING MATTER RELATING TO THE GENERAL SUBJECT.

———— • —◆—• ————

MONTGOMERY, ALA.:
BARRETT & WIMBISH, BOOK AND GENERAL JOB PRINTERS.

1859.

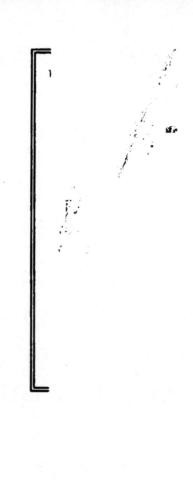

INTRODUCTION.

Most of the letters which are contained in this little volume were written by Gen. Woodward, without any idea of their being presented to the public in this form. Indeed, the first two, addressed to his friend Mr. Hanrick, were not expected to be published, at all; but being casually shown to the writer of this introduction, he solicited and obtained them for insertion in the columns of the Montgomery Mail, believing that their contents would prove attractive to a large class of readers who feel much interest in all that concerns the early history of the State. Subsequently, Gen. Woodward was kind enough to contribute to the "Mail," (with which the undersigned is connected as senior editor,) a number of letters containing much valuable matter relative to the history, customs, &c., of the Creek Confederacy of Indian tribes. About the same time, friends of his caused the publication, in the Columbus Sun and Union Springs Gazette, of several letters written by Gen. W. to them. All these letters, replete as they were with incidents and descriptions of a most interesting character, found favor with the public ; and the undersigned was frequently applied to for copies of them, which it was impossible to supply. This suggested to him the idea of publishing the whole in a form convenient both for preservation and reference. He therefore immediately wrote to Gen. Woodward asking his consent to his having the letters collectively published. It was with some difficulty that this consent was obtained, as Gen. Woodward alleged that his want of early education and the inaccuracy of his style unfitted him to appear before the public as a writer of historical sketches. He only yielded, at length, to the argument that he alone, perhaps, of living men, possessed a knowledge of the many interesting facts and traditions he had acquired during an intercouse of nearly half a century with the Indian tribes of the South-west. These facts are stated in justice to Gen. Woodward and with the view of disarming the hypercritical, who might be disposed to be severe upon the homely but effective phraseology with which the General's interesting narrations are clothed.

One or two of the letters addressed to the late lamented Col. Albert J. Pickett, who did his State so much service and himself so much credit, by his elaborate *History of Alabama*, were never seen by that gentleman. They were received for publication by the writer of this, about the time of Col. Pickett's last illness. In one of his letters in this volume, Gen. Woodward pays a sincere tribute to the memory of his old friend. In the same letter, he speaks his admiration of and regard for two other prominent Alabamians, lately deceased : ex-Gov. Arthur P. Bagby, and Col. Charles McLemore, of Chambers county.

It is more than twenty years since the writer first saw and knew Gen. Woodward. His personal acquaintance with him was but slight ; yet he knew well his reputation in East Alabama, as a brave, rough, warm-hearted man, of fine intellectual endowments, a most sagacious judge of character, exten-sive knowledge of Creek Indian history, manners and character—with an in-domitable will and a sturdy self-reliance, which spoke for itself in his tall, sinewy form and strongly-marked, expressive face. A discriminating observ-er, at that time, would have selected him out of a thousand, as the man most fertile in resources, most indomitable in the execution of his plans, and pos-sessing in the highest degree the physical qualities most needed in the emer-gencies and hardships of a semi-Indian life. His exterior was rough, his manners military and at times abrupt, but those who knew him best, were well aware that he had a heart large enough for any deed of real benevolence. The presuming or pretentious he mercilessly flayed with a biting sarcasm, of which he was master; and many anecdotes are told, illustrative of his powers of repartee. But to the weak and unprotected, he was and is invariably con-siderate and kind. In proof of this, it may be mentioned here, that when he learned thro' Col. Banks, of Columbus, Ga., that Mrs. Dill, (whom he and others rescued from the Indians in Florida, in 1818,) was still living at or near Fort Gaines, he immediately transmitted, thro' the writer of this, a sum of money to Col. Banks, for the relief of the old lady's necessities.

Few men have had better opportunities for studying the Indian character and investigating their customs, than Gen. Woodward. Very early in life, as appears from two autobiographical letters which were received at so late a day as to compel their insertion in the Appendix to this little volume, he was brought into contact with the Red Man; and, stirred by the Indian blood in his own viens, he studied his character and traditions lovingly and earnestly. His early appointment to the command of a body of friendly Indians, in time of war, proves that he was considered to know them and to have influence over them.

As to the consideration in which Gen. Woodward was held by his superiors, it is not improper to state that the writer of this has now in his possession an original letter from Gen. Jackson, speaking of Gen. W., as "a brave, intrepid and gallant soldier." It bears date, "Nashville, September 30, 1819."

It is a matter of great regret to the writer, that many errors have una-voidably crept into the publication. The difficulty of decyphering Indian and other proper names has been the chief cause. Some of the principal are "*Danville*" instead of Greenville, on page 5; "*Anderson*" Dexter instead of Andrew Dexter, on same page; "*Vaugh*" instead of Vaughn, on page 9; on same page, "lettered *Birch*" instead of Beech; on page 16, "*Polander*" instead of Hollander; and on page 25, "*Simonides*" instead of Seminoles.

In conclusion, the writer of this would remark, that he believes that the unpretending pages which follow contain a very great deal of matter of high historical value to the people of Alabama and Georgia. For that reason, he has taken the trouble to collect such of the Letters as had been published previously and to induce Gen. Woodward to write others. For the task of arranging, pruning, etc., he has had neither time nor health; but he trusts that even in their present crude form, they may effect much good, in the cor-rection of several popular errors and in familiarising our people with the later history of those tribes that have recently departed from our borders.

Montgomery, Ala., Jan. 15, 1859.   J. J. HOOPER.

REMINISCENCES.

———••———

WHEELING, WINN PARISH, LA.⎱
May 2, 1857. ⎰

E. HANRICK, ESQ.—*My Old Friend:* The Montgomery
Mail comes occasionally directed to me at tiis office; and,
wietier tie paper is paid for or not, I am unable to say,
tiougi I requested a gentleman to do so, and ie says tie
money was forwarded. If suci is not tie case, call on
tie Editor and pay wiat is due, and also pay for another
year's subscription, and write to me at tiis office, and
you siall have your money immediately. It is tirougi
tie Mail I frequently iear you are living, whici I hope
will be the case for many years to come. My friend, how
time and things have changed since first we met! I think
it has been forty years, tie last winter, since I first saw
you, at Granville, Pitt county, N. C., rolling tar barrels.
And your city, Montgomery, about that time, or siortly
after, was started, or begun, by Anderson Dexter, and
now, I suppose, is one of tie most desirable spots in tie
Soutiwest. I knew the spot wiere Montgomery stands
before any wiite man ever tiougit of locating tiere.
When I look back on tiings as tiey then were and wiat
they are now, it makes me feel—as I am—old. You
and I iave lived in fast times, wiich our ieads will siow,
my friend; so, let it rock on—we will only sleep the
sounder when it comes to our time to rest. I also see
announced in the Mail tie deati of several old friends,
among tiem Gen. Shackeltord, wiom I have known from
my boyiood. I was witi iim in Florida, in 1812, in an

expedition against the Seminoles. There are but few of
that detachment of Georgians now living—in fact, I know
of none, unless it be Dr. Fort, of Macon, Ga., John H.
Howard, of Columbus, Ga., Col. R. Broadnax, of Ala.,
and myself. If there are any more of them, it is very few,
and I have lost the hang of them; but, should I live, I
will be in Milledgeville, Ga., on the first day of July,
1862, which will be fifty years from the time we started
on that expedition. If you are then living in Montgomery, I will give you a call.

I also see that my old friend, Major Thomas M. Cowles,
is no more. He was a good man—I knew him before he
was a man. He was fit to live in any country that God
may think proper to occupy with honest men. He belonged to my staff, and accompanied me to Fort Mitchell,
with an escort under the command of Gen. Wm. Taylor,
to conduct Gen. LaFayette to Montgomery. I shall
never forget a visit that Major Cowles and myself paid to
Billy Weatherford, the Quadroon, him about whom so
much has been said and so little known. We remained
some days, and among our crowd were Zach. McGirth,
Davy Tait, the half-brother to Weatherford, old Sam.
Moniac, who, many years before, had accompanied Alex.
McGillivray to New York, in General Washington's time.
I have often thought that I would give you and friend
Hooper, of the Mail, a little sketch of what I had learned
from those men and others, in relation to Indian matters;
but they are all dead, and what I have heard and know,
would, in many instances, contradict what has gone to the
world as history, and I do not know that mankind would
be better off, even if I could undeceive and give them
what I do know in relation to Indian history, and so I
will let it pass. But, still, there is one thing I want, if it
can be got hold of, and, if George Stiggins is living in
your country, he has it. It is a manuscript given to me
by the widow of Col. Hawkins. It is in the hand-writing
of Christian Limbo, who lived with Col. Hawkins many
years. It was copied from Col. Hawkins' own manuscript,

which was burned shortly after his death. I knew Col. Hawkins well. He knew more about Indians and Indian history, and early settlements and expeditions of the several European nations that undertook to settle colonies in the South and Southwest, than all the men that ever have or will make a scrape of a pen upon the subject. The loss of his papers was certainly a very great loss to those who would wish to know things as they really were, and not as they wished them. Stiggins, you know, had some learning, and and was a half breed of the Netchis tribe, tho' raised among the Creeks. He spoke of writing a history of the Creeks and other Southern tribes, and I loaned him my papers. I presume he has done by this time what he contemplated, and please see him and get my papers, if you can, and take care of them until you have a chance to send them to me. You will also find among the papers some in my hand-writing, that I intended for a Mr. Daniel K. Whitaker, of Charleston, S. C., who was concerned in a Southern literary journal.

*   *   *   *   *   *   *   *   *

Yours, truly, old friend,
THOS. S. WOODARD.

WHEELING, WINN PARISH, LA., }
December 9, 1857. }

E. HANRICK, ESQ.:

My Old Friend:—Your letter came to hand safe, after taking its time, as I have, in going through the world, quite leisurely. You will find five dollars enclosed: pay yourself, and hand the other two and a half to the editor of the Mail: say to him, that after he has worked that out, and he learns that I have not *worked out*, he may continue to send his paper. I see my letter to you, of May last, in the Mail. The editor speaks in very flattering terms of my capability in giving sketches and making them accurate and interesting. I would be proud that I could do so, and prove to his readers that he was not mistaken. It is true, I have known Alabama a great while, and many of its earliest settlers—particularly Indians and Indian countrymen. And I would most willingly, if I thought any facts that have come within my knowledge, or circumstances related to me by others in whom I could place the most implicit reliance, would be interesting to the readers of the Mail, give them. But as I write no better than in my younger days, but much worse; and as anything I might write would to most persons be of little interest, I must now abandon it. Besides, you know my capacity for embellishment (the only thing that suits too many readers,) is not such as would render my sketches very interesting to many. I have no doubt but that, if I could be with you, and many more old acquaintances that I left in Alabama, (and hope they still live,) and could get around a lightwood fire, I could interest you— or, at least, spin over old times and bring many things to your recollection that you have forgotten. (I do not allude to old store accounts. Though you have lost many, I never heard of your forgetting one.)

I often wish myself back in Alabama, and have as often regretted leaving Tuskegee. I was the founder of Tuskegee. I selected the place for the county site, or place for the court house, in 1833. I built the first house on that ridge, though James Dent built the first house on the court house square, after the lots were laid off. The day I made the selection, there was a great ball-play with the Tuskegees, Chunnanuggees, Chehaws and Tallesees. A Col. Deas, a South Carolinian, was with me. Ned, those were good days, were they not? I can never recall them, nor many other things that were very cheering to me then. I wonder if my five cedar trees, that I planted at the McGarr place when I owned it, are living yet? Ned, I, in company with my family, old Aunt Betsy Kurnells, (or Connells,) Tuskencha, and old John Mc-Queen, dug up those cedars, when they were very small,

from under a large cedar that shaded the birth-place of
Ussa Yoholo, or, Black Drink, who, after the murder of
General Thompson, in Florida, was known to the world
as Oceola. This man was the great grand-son of James
McQueen. You knew his father—the little Englishman,
Powell. His mother was Polly Copinger. The rail road
from Montgomery to West Point runs within five feet,
if not over the place, where the cabin stood in which
Billy Powell, or Ussa Yoholo, was born. The old cedar
was destroyed by Gen. McIver's negroes, when grading
the road. It was in an old field, between the Nufaupba
(what is now called Ufaupee), and a little creek that the
Indians called Catsa Bogah, which mouths just below
where the rail road crosses Nufaupba; and on the Montgomery side of Nufaupba, and on a plantation owned by
a Mr. Vaugh, when I left the country, rests the remains
of old James McQueen, a Scotchman, who died in 1811,
aged—from what Col. Hawkins and many others said he
was—128 years. He informed Col. Hawkins that he was
born 1683, and came into the Creek nation in 1716, a de-
serter from an English vessel anchored at St. Augustine,
East Florida, for striking a naval officer. When I planted those cedars, I had a wife and three children. I
thought, then, to make at the foot of one of them a resting place. But more than twenty years have elapsed,
and many changes have taken place with me and those
that were with me then, and I care but little now when
or where I may be picked up. But still, I would be glad
to know that the cedars were spared; for, none who knew
the hands of those that assisted me in planting them there,
could think of molesting them—unless, there should be
one with a marring hand, like him that destroyed the
old lettered birch at the old Federal crossing of the Persimmon creek, and the old Council Oak that once stood in
front of Suckey Kurnells' or Connells' house, which you
knew well. Yes, it was under that oak, where you and
I have heard many a good yarn spun, both by our white
as well as red friends—many of whom have long since

gone to that world of which we read and talk so much, and so much dreaded by many, (if not more,) and which never can be known to living man. Yes, friend, it was under that oak—held as sacred by the Indians, and should have been as memorable among Alabamians, as the old Charter Oak of New England was, among the people of the North—where you and I have aided in placing the brand of Molly Thompson upon many a black bottle. I rented out the plantation one year, while I owned it, and forbid the tree being touched. The man renting it complained so much about its shading his crops, I allowed either three or five dollars for it, I now forget which, and would now pay $100 to have it living, as it was when I left the place, were it possible to restore it. You have often heard our mutual friend, old Capt. Billy Walker, tell about him and myself, camping there with Cols. Hawkins, Barnett and McDonald, of the army, and Gen. John Sevier, one of the heroes of King's Mountain. (Col. Barnett was the father of Tom. and Nat. Barnett.) On the side of the Indians there were Billy McIntosh, Big Warrior, Alex. Kurnells, and many others. Kurnells was the interpreter, wearing that Iroquois coat you have often seen in the possession of the big woman, his wife. On that occasion, Kurnells exhibited many Indian curiosities; among them was the buck's horn, resembling a man's hand, which you have seen in my possession since. Some years ago I gave the horn to Bishop Soule, of Nashville. There is not an Indian in the Creek nation that ever visited Alex. Kurnell's, but would recognize the horn as quick as you would your horse shoe. Gen. Sevier lived but a few days after this, and his remains lie in the hill near old Fort Decatur; but not a stone or board marks the resting place of the patriot, which is the case with hundreds of others that lived in his day, and like himself, served their country for their country's good, and not their own.

This is becoming tedious to you, no doubt, and I must stop. But you can excuse it, as I live alone and have so little to employ my time about, that my mind is often led to contemplate things that have passed and would have been forgotten, but for my lonely situation. It affords me some satisfaction to think and talk, (when I meet an old friend,) of old times; and after commencing to write, these old things *would* appear, and I felt bound to give them some attention.

Yours,

T. S. W

Winn Parish, La., Dec. 24 1857.

J. J. Hooper, Esq.:

I wrote a letter to my old friend, E. Hanrick, of Montgomery, last May, in which I spoke of giving you some few sketches of Indians and their history. Why I alluded to these things, I had a short time before seen an extract in your paper taken, I think, from a Mobile paper, making some inquiry about the true meaning or the signification of *Alabama*. And from the article, I supposed the writer to think that the word *Alabama* was of the Jewish origin, by giving the name of Esau's wife, who spelt her name Al-i-ba-ma, (if she could spell.) Now whether she borrowed her name from Jedediah Morse, or he the name from her, it matters not, as both spell it alike. The word Alabama, and many other words among the Indians, as well as customs, have been seized upon by some to establish a fact that never existed: that is, to prove that the North American Indians descended from the Lost Tribes of Israel. Now it would be as easy to prove that such tribes never existed, and much easier to prove that they dwindled away among those Eastern nations that frequently held them in bondage, than to prove that anything found in the native Indian is characteristic of the Jew. I have traveled among a great many tribes, and circumcision is unknown to them; and besides, an Indian in his native state is proverbial for his honesty, and from the records handed to us as authentic, the great Author of all nature was put to much trouble to keep the Jews and the property of their neighbors in their proper places.

I will return to my letter. I see it published in an October number of your paper, and shortly after its appearance, I received a letter from a Mr. J. D. Driesbach, of Baldwin Co., Ala., requesting me to give him what information I could of the persons whose names were mentioned in my letter to Mr. Hanrick, and any thing I knew of Indians and their history that I thought would be interesting; also, informing me that he had seen in the possession of Joseph Stiggins, the son of Geo. Stiggins, a manuscript of George Stiggins, which had been loaned to Col. Pickett when he wrote the History of Alabama: and whether interesting or not, I scribbled off some twenty or thirty pages and sent to him, and among other things I gave him what I understood to be the origin of *Alabama*, as we have it from the Indians. I find in Col. Pickett's answer to Mr. Hobbs, that he agrees with me how Alabama took its name. I am satisfied that Col. Pickett is correct. I also stated to Mr. Driesbach, that I had heard Col. Hawkins say in his time, that he had made every inquiry in his power to ascertain if *Alabama* had any other meaning than the mere name of an Indian town, but never could, unless the name—as it was possible— might be the Indian corruption of the Spanish words for *good water*, though he doubted that.

Col. Pickett is correct, as to the Alabama Town being just below Montgomery, for I was at it when they lived there, and it was called Ecanchatty, from the red bluffs on which a portion of Montgomery is built. The Tarwassaw Town was a little lower down the river than the Colonel has it, though it is a matter of no importance. The Autauga, or what the Indians called Autauga or Dumplin Town, was at the place where Washington is in Antanga county. The Alabamas, and those little towns connected with them, extended down the river as far as Beach

creek, that mouths just above Sclma, and up the river to
where Coosawda is—on the Autanga side. To spell it
the way the Indians pronounced it, and the way Col. Hawkins spelt, is Coowarsartda. The Alabamas differed from
the Musqua or Muscogees, as do the Choctaws from the
Chickasaws; but were what the Indians call the "same
fire-side" people. There was much of their dialect that
differed from that of the common Creek, or Musqua, as
the Western Indians used to call them, and no doubt
once they were a different tribe.

About the close of the American Revolution, a large
portion of the Alabamas and Coowarsartdas returned to
Texas on the Trinity, being under the control of a Chief
called Red Shoes, or Stillapikachatta. I visited these
Indians in 1816, in company with Mr. Angus Gilchrist
and Mr. Edward McLauchlin. Mr. McLauchlin was the
best Indian interpreter I ever knew, except Hamly, who
was raised by Forbes and Panthon, in Florida. Red
Shoes was then living, and lived for years after. I inquir-
ed much into his history and that of his people. He gave
the same account of their being driven from their old
homes in the West and their settlement in Alabama and a
part of Georgia, as has been given me by the Creeks.
And if Indian tradition and what I have heard from Col.
Hawkins—who, I think, was the most sensible man I ever
was acquainted with, and whose opportunities were as
good if not much better than any one else of his day possessed, to collect correct information in relation to the
early settlements of the Creeks and their confederates in
Alabama and Georgia—are to be relied on, Col. Pickett
must have been wrongly informed as to the fights with
the Muscogees and Alabamas upon the sources of Red
river, as well as to the Muscogees settling in Ohio, the
Alabamas settling on the Yazoo, and the destruction of
their fort by DeSoto, and the Alabamas being the first to
settle in what is now known to us as the Creek country.

It has always been a contested point, with the Indians,
whether Tuckabatchee, or old Cusetaw opposite Fort

Mitchell on the Chattahoochee river, was settled first·
but it is generally conceded that Cusetaw was settled
first. These two towns have, in almost every instance,
furnished the head Chiefs of the nation: Tuckabatchee
furnishing the upper town Chief—Cusetaw, the lower
town Chief. This fact is well known .to all who have
been well acquainted with the Creeks. Besides, John
Ferdinand Soto, who by most persons has been called
Ilernanda DeSoto, after landing his forces in Florida,
passed through a portion of Georgia, and across the entire
State of Alabama, before he could have reached the
Yazoo in Mississippi. And in addition to this, one of
the severest battles Soto had with the Indians, was fought
with the Creeks at what is now known as Cuwally. It is
either in Montgomery or Tallapoosa county; I do not
now know how the county lines run. Cuwally is a name
given it by the whites, not knowing how to give it the
Indian pronunciation. To spell it as the Indians pronounced it, it would be Thleawalla, which signifies *rolling
bullet.* Thlea, is an arrow or bullet; walla, is to roll. The
Indians say it was there that a spent ball was seen rolling
on the ground, and from that the place took its name.
Besides, the Tuckabatchees have now in their possession
a number of plates of copper in various shapes, which the
Spaniards used as a kind of sheld, to protect themselves
from the arrows of the Indians. These plates were taken
from the Spaniards at that fight. And from what Col.
Pickett says of the fights upon the sources of Red River it
would appear that the Indians were some years on their
route going East. I have not seen nor heard any tradition-
ary account of any thing of the sort in my intercourse
with the various tribes that I have been among, and the
sources of Red River must have been very imperfectly
known in that day, by any of the Europeans that had
visited this country, and are still very imperfectly known
by many of our own people to this day; for Red river
does not, as believed by many, head in the Rocky Mountains, but is a mere leak or drain from the prairies, except

those little streams that head in the Ozark hills of Arkansas. Besides, it is not such a country as Indians would likely stop long in, particularly traveling on foot, as they were obliged to do; for the Southwestern Indians knew nothing of horses until they were introduced into the country by the Spaniards. And building forts with logs, by a people who knew nothing of the uses of the axe, nor had any, would, I think, be a tough undertaking. All that I have seen and heard satisfies me at least, that the Creeks, Alabamas and the other little bands connected with them, originally inhabited the skirts of timbered country between the Rio Grande or Del Norte and the Mississippi river, near the Gulf coast, which the names of the creeks, rivers, and many other things, will show. The Choctaws, Chickasaws, Nitches, Nacogdoches and Natchitoches Indians inhabited pretty much the same country.

It is true that Cortez found a much more civilized and much more timid race to contend with, than any of the tribes that I have mentioned. And that the Creeks, Alabamas and others that I have named, ever were or considered themselves subjects of the great Mexican Empire, I am very much inclined to doubt, from what I know of them. Even the present civilized and christianized rulers of Mexico, who are almost to a man of the old race, never exercise any control over the Indians within her borders, and this has been the case ever since she got from under the Spanish yoke.

I can neither read French nor Spanish; but the few translations in English that I have seen taken from the travels of the early visitors, both of the French and Spanish, to this country, are very contradictory, and for that reason I have been inclined to credit the Indian tradition. And, even if a history taken from European travelers, somewhat in the shape of a novel, is to be relied on, some man, in his account of the conquest of Florida, admits that the Creeks, Muscogees or Coosas disputed the passage of Soto through the country—that is, Alabama and Georgia. It

has been a long time since I read it, and then but little;
but if I am not mistaken, it spoke of a war, or battle,
with a Chief called Tuscaloosa. The Creeks themselves
said that there was once among them a giant Chief, Tustanugga Lusta, or Black Warrior, who fought with Soto, and
that his home was on the river of that name. I have seen
no history of Louisiana except the Tax Collectors' Book—
and that I dislike to read—and cannot say at what time
Biennville and his brother, Iberville, came to the country.
But one thing is certain, the French knew something of
Mobile and its immediate vicinity at an early day; but
they knew very little of the interior of Alabama until
after the defeat of Gen. Braddock, near Pittsburg, which
which was in 1755. The next year they come down the
Ohio and Mississippi rivers and drove the Nitches Indians
from where the present city of Natchez, Miss., now is.
The Nitches Indians immediately emigrated to join their
old Western friends, the Creeks, and settle at the Talisee
old fields, on Taliseehatchy or Talisee creek, now in Talladega county, Ala.; and the French very shortly after
moved up the Alabama river, to the junction of Coosa
and Tallapoosa rivers, and built a little village near to old
Fort Jackson. I have seen Indians, as well as negroes,
that traded with the French while there, though their
stay was but a few years. James McQueen, a Scotchman—the first white man I ever heard of being among
the Creeks—and a Polander, by the name of Moniac,
with the Nitches Indians and Creeks, broke up the French
settlement at the fork of the rivers. And it was on the
return of the French down the Alabama river, that they
threw up an entrenchment at Durand's or Durant's Bend,
and another at the mouth of Cahawba—and the Alabama
Indians were said to be the most bitter enemies, except
the Nitches, that the French had. We are to judge from
Col. Pickett's version of the matter, that there were
neither Alabamas nor Muscogees in what is known to the
whites as the Creek country, before Soto passed through.
The Chattahoochee Indians, who were Muscogees, would

show, as long as they lived there, many places where DeSoto or Soto had camped. There is a place on the Apalachicola that is yet known as one of Soto's camps. The Indians call it Spanny Wakka—that is, "the Spaniards lay there." The Indians could tell of the old Spanish fortification in Jones county, Ga., also the one on the Ocmulgee, above Fort Hawkins, and it is evident they must have been in the country before Soto passed through—and, besides, I was in Florida in 1818, and had with me many of the Creeks, who could point out places where the Spaniards, under Soto, had camped, and the marks of old roads and causeways were then visible. And with the single exception of Soto himself, all the early explorers of that country, who were mostly Spanish and some French, would only ascend the navigable rivers a small distace, in water crafts constructed for the purpose, and could have known but little of the Indians in the interior. And as to Red River, when Cortez conquered Mexico, it is a doubt with me if it was then a tributary of the Mississippi river, as the Atchafalaya evidently was once the channel of Red River, and made its way to the Gulf of Mexico through Berwick's Bay; and, even in Soto's time did it go into the Mississippi river, it could only have been navigated, with small crafts, as far up as Alexandria, for the river above the falls will show that it was once a raft, as far up as Long Prairie, in Arkansas, and that would have prevented early explorers from knowing much of the sources of the river or what Indians, if any, lived on it.

All these circumstances induce me to believe that Col. Pickett is mistaken, and the source from which he derived a part of his information is, or was, not very reliable; and, so far as Indian tradition is concerned, I think my chance to have obtained correct information in relation to Indian history equal, at least, to that of Col. Pickett's. The accounts that I have had from the Indians themselves, and from Col. Hawkins, whose opportunity must have been as good as any one of his time, or any one who has

lived since, are, that Cortez's object was gold, and that the
people he first encountered in Mezico were somewhat
civilized and very timid; and, after subduing them and
taking possession of the City of Mexico—if it could be
called a city—he then commenced extending his con-
quests or robberies up the Gulf coast, in the direction of
what is now Tampico and Tamaulipas, and even as far as
what is now Texas, where he encountered the Musquas
or Muscogees, Alabamas, and others that I have mentioned; but finding them to be a much more hardy, war-
like race than the Mexicans, and in order to hold on to
what he had taken and subdued of the timid ones, he
found it necessary to kill or drive these war-like tribes
from the country, which with the great advantage of fire-
arms, he succeeded in doing. The Muscogees and their
confederates crossed the Mississippi river and called a
halt at Baton Rouge, which is known to this day as Red
Stick or Club. The Nitches, from the river which bears
their name in Texas, crossed the Mississippi river and
settled where the city of Natchez is now. The Choctaws
settled the country on Yazoo, Pearl, Leaf, Chickasawha,
and as far as the Tombecba rivers. The Chickasaws settled at Chickasaw Bluff or Memphis. The Creeks, after
a short stay at Baton Rouge, moved and settled on the
Alabama and its tributaries, the Black Warrior and the
Chattahoochee, and Flint rivers, and, in time, went as far
east as the Oconee river, but never went farther in that
direction, and did not make any settlement on the Oconee
until after the whites began to encroach on the Indians of
that country from the East. The Indians that originally
inhabited from the middle parts of the Carolinas (partien-
larly South Carolina,) and Georgia to the seaboard, were
known as Yamacraws or Yamasees, Oconees, Ogeeches,
and Sowanokees or People of the Glades. The Sowanokees are known as the Shawnees—the other Indians
know them by no other name to this day but Sowanokee;
and the Savannah river was known as Sowanokee
Hatchee Thlocka, which signifies the Big River of the

Glades, or what we call Savannah. And these Indians the Creeks found to be their equals as warriors; but when the whites began to approach them from the east, and the Creeks already very close on the west, the Sowanokees or Shawnees fell back on the north and northwest. Tecumseh was of that stock. The other little tribes, with the Uchees, they being the "same fireside" Indians with the Shawnees, all dwindled away among the Creeks and lost their language, except the Uchees—they still retain theirs.

One other circumstance that convinces me that the Creeks and Alabamas had become pretty much one people before they settled Alabama and Georgia, is that the tribes they incorporated into their nation after settling the Creek country never would come into the family arrangement, which arrangement I will try and explain to you. They were laid off in families—that is, Bears, Wolves, Panthers, Foxes, and many others—also, what they termed the Wind Family, which was allowed more authority than any family in the nation. There was nothing in their laws to prevent blood cousins from marrying, but never to marry in the same family—thus, a man of the Bear family could marry a woman of the Fox family, or any other family he pleased, and the children would be called Fox. In all cases, the children took the mother's family name. Years ago, you could not find an Indian in the nation but could tell you his family. But whisky has destroyed many of their old customs as well as the Indians themselves.

There is too much of this to publish, even if it were worth publishing. Read it, show it to Col. Pickett, burn it and send me his History of Alabama. Yours,

T. S. W.

To J. J. HOOPER, ESQ.:

I wrote to you some time back some sketches relative to the Creek Indians, which no doubt you found too long, too tedious, and too uninteresting to publish. In that I sent you I made mention of a family arrangement among the Creeks that differed from all other tribes that I know or have traveled among. The Creeks are laid off in families, viz: Bears, Tigers, Wolves, Foxes, Deers, and almost all the animals that were known to them. All these families had certain privileges, and every one of a family knew to what family he belonged and what privileges were allowed. There was also what they termed the Wind family, which was allowed more privileges than than all the rest. For instance, when an offender escaped from justice, all the families were permitted to pursue a certain number of days, and no more, except the Wind family, which had the right to pursue and arrest at any time—there was no limit to their privileges in bringing an offender to justice. There was nothing to prevent blood relations from marrying with each other, but a woman of the Bear family was at liberty te take a husband in any family except a Bear; so it was with all the other families, but none were permitted to marry in the same family; for instance, if a man of the Wolf family marry a woman of the Fox family, the children would all be Foxes. Such has been the custom among the Creeks from the earliest history I have had of them, though their intercourse with the whites has changed many of their old habits and customs even since my time. In fact, I know a number of words in their language and names of things and places that are not spoken or pronounced as they were when I first knew them. This has been occasioned by the whites not being able to give the Indian

pronunciation, and the Indians in many cases have con-
formed to that of the whites. A horse, for instance, is
now called Chelocko by the whites who speak Indian, and
by most of the Indians; but originally it was Echo Tlocko,
signifying a Big Deer—Echo is a deer and Thlocko is
something large. The first horses the Creeks ever saw
were those introduced by the Spaniards, and they called
them big deer, as they resembled that animal more than any
other they knew—this is their tradition, and I am satisfied that it is correct. There is the Indian town above
Montgomery, Coowersartda, that is called by the whites
Coosada; also the town Thleawalla, where Soto fought
the Creeks, it is called by the whites Cuwally, and many
of the Indians raised of late years call it as the whites do,
and do not know what its original name was, nor what
its meaning is. Thlea is an arrow or bullet, and Walla
is to roll; the proper name is Rolling Bullet; and many
other such alterations have been made that have come
within my knowledge. Indians in almost every instance
learn our language quicker that we learn theirs, particu-
larlarly our pronunciation. An Indian, if he speaks our
language at all, almost invariably pronounces it as those
do frc m whom he learns it. If he learns it from a white
man that speaks it well, the Indian does the same; if he
learns it from a negro he pronounces as the negro does. You
may take the best educated European that lives, that does
not speak our language, and an Indian that does not
speak it; let both learn it; if the Indian does not learn
so much, he will always speak what he does learn more
distinctly than the European. This will no doubt be disputed by many, but I know it to be true from actual ob-
servation, and I do not pretend to account for why it is
so, unless it is intended that at some time Americans shall
all be Americans.

I believe I mentioned the name of James McQueen before. This man came amongst the Creeks as early as
1716 and lived among them until 1811. He was said to
be, by those who knew him well, very intelligent, and

2

had taken great pains to make himself acquainted with
the history of the Creeks. From the early day in which
he came among them, and they knowing at that time but
little of the whites, their traditions were, no doubt, much
more reliable than anything that can now be obtained
from them. From what I have learned from this man,
or from those who learned it from him, the Muscogees,
or as they were originally known to the other tribes,
Musquas, and all the little towns or bands that composed the Creek Confederacy, was a Confederacy before
they crossed to the east of Mississippi river. From
what I have been able to learn, Musqua, or Muscogee,
signified Independent. Besides I knew a Capt. John S.
Porter, formerly of the U. S. Army, who, some thirty
years ago, with a few Creeks of the McIntosh party in
Arkansas, visited California and went up the Pacific coast
to the Columbia river, and returned by the way of Salt
Lake, and on his return to Arkansas he wrote to me,
giving an account of his travels. The writing covered
some three or four sheets of paper; a great deal of it was
very interesting. I do not now recollect whether I loaned
it to George Stiggins, or a Mr. Whitaker, of Charleston,
S. C. But I recollect among the many accounts of his
travels, that on the head waters, or at least the waters of
the Colorado of the West, he found a small remnant of
the original Musqua. They spoke mostly a broken Spanish dialect, but still retained much of their old language
and old family customs. They gave pretty much the
same account of being driven from their old homes that
I have learned from the Creeks. These people informed
Capt. Porter that their nation was once strong, and they
had many languages; that they inhabited the country
between the Rio del Norte and Mississippi river, or Owea
Coafka, or river of cane. They also gave him the original
Indian name of the Del Norte, but I forget it; but Owea
Coafka is what the Creeks call the Mississippi river.
They also stated to him that they lived near the Gulf, on
what they called Owea Thlocko Marhe, signifying the

largest water. They say they were driven off by the Echo
Thlock Ulgees, or horsemen, or what the Creeks in our
lauguage would call the big deer men. Echothlock is a
big deer, as I stated before, and the proper name of the
horse Echothlock; Ulgee* means horsemen. They also
stated that long after they left their old homes, and horses
had become plenty, that the Indians learned the use of
them, and that a number of the little tribes that once
lived on the rivers and Gulf had taken to the prairies.
They also gave Capt. Porter an account of a long war
with some tribes high up on the Rio del Norte, and that
one of the most warlike tribes had gone east. They called them as the present Creeks do, Hopungieasaw, and
what are now known to the whites as Pyankeshaws. I
recollect two women that Tuskenea carried to the Creek
nation, of the Pyankeshaws, as the whites called them,
but the Creeks call them Hopungieasaw, or dancing Indians.

You see that I differ with Col. Pickett as to the early
settlement of the Creek Indians in Alabama; and should
I be correct, it need not matter with the Colonel, for you
know most people believe a history whether it be correct
or not. I have not seen his History of Alabama, and all
I have seen or heard from him, was his answer to Mr.
Hobbs' inquiry; and I have no idea that he has written
anything but he felt authorized to do from the sources
that he received his information. But authors sometimes
may err, and others wilfully misrepresent. When that is
the case, we have to judge from circumstances. The
Colonel says that Soto passed Alabama before the Muscogees reached that country. The Indians say they were
there and fought him: and from the number of copper
shields, with a small brass swivel, (that an old man by the
name of Tooley worked up into bells,) would go to show
and to prove that the Indians were correct. I have often
seen the copper plates or shields, and a piece of the swivel, and from the cuttings or carvings on it, it was évident-

* *Ulgæe* is rather a Creek termination which applies the antecedent
description to a *person* or *persons*. It answers to our *ian*. A Creek
would call a Carolin*ian* a Carolin*ulgee*.   H.

ly of Spanish make. And it was only some twenty years
after Cortez conquered Mexico, that Soto commenced his
march from Tampa Bay, and had too few men to sacri-
fice them in storming a strong work, when it could effect
nothing, for an Indian Fort in a remote wilderness could
have interfered but little with his march westward. And
how could the Alabamas have known that he intended
passing that way ? It seems to me that a people so illy
prepared to build forts; having no axes, spades nor any
implement of the sort, would have found it much easier to
have concealed themselves, had it been necessary, in some
of those large swamps which abound in the Yazoo country;
and from what I know of Indians, they would not give
one swamp or cane brake for forty forts. And as to the
Muscogees ever having been subjects of the great Mexican empire, it is very doubtful, for Mexico was the name
of the City itself, and applied to the town only. It was
the city or town where the principal chiefs or body of the
Aztecs, Anahuacs, or as the other Indians called them,
Auchinang resided.

The Creeks or Muscogees, the Iroquois or Six Nations,
were all the Indians that I have known or heard of forming themselves into anything like a confederacy. The
balance, as far as my information extends, have been separate tribes, with a separate language, with their own peculiar customs, except in a few instances where two or
more tribes would unite in case of a war. The Creeks,
as I mentioned before, originally inhabited the skirts of
timbered country bordering on the Gulf of Mexico, and
between the Del Norte and Mississippi rivers. When the
Muscogees, Nitches, Choctaws and Chickasaws crossed
to the east of the Mississippi river, a town of Indians yet
among the Creeks, the Autisees or Otisees, has for ages
been called Red Stick. They settled at Baton Rouge,
and no doubt it was from that tribe or town that the
early French settlers gave it its present name. Eto-chatty,
signifies red tree or red wood; but ask an Indian that is
acquainted with the original names and customs, what a

Red Stick Warrior is, and he will tell you it is an Autisee or Otisee. I have taken great pains, in times passed, to have these things explained to me by the oldest and most sensible Indians and Indian countrymen. The Muscogees, from their own account, made but a short stay on the Mississippi or its waters. They emigrated to Alabama and Georgia, and settled mostly on the large creeks and rivers and near the falls and shoals, for the purpose of fishing. The Indians who inhabited the Gulf coast, and that of the Atlantic as far east as Beaufort, S. C., and the rivers as far back as latitude 33° north, previous to the settlement of the Muscogees in the country, were known as Paspagolas, Baluxies, Movilas, Apilaches, Hichetas, Uchys, Yemacraws, Wimosas, Sowanokas or Shawneys. Sowanoka Hatchy is the original name of Savannah river · that is, the river of the glades.

The Simondes is a mixed race of almost all the tribes I have mentioned, but mostly Hitchetas and Creeks. The Hitchetas have by the whites been looked upon as being originally Muscogees, but they were not. They had an entirely different language of their own, and were in the country when the Creeks first entered it. Simoude, in the Creek language, signifies wild, or runaway, or outlaw.

There have many conflicting accounts about John Ferdinand Soto—when, where and how he died, and where buried. According to McQueen's account, and that of the oldest Indians in the nation when he came to it, Soto died in what is called Natchitochees parish, in this State, at the last fort he built, called the Azadyze; and the oldest Spanish settlers of this country have corroborated McQueen's account. There are yet to be found among the people of this country, some of the descendants of Soto's men, and some of his name. All the Indian traditions, and those of the early Spanish settlers, say he died and was buried at Azadyze. It is now 142 years since McQueen first came to the Creek country, and Indians that were then living even at the age of 75 years, could give a very correct tradition of things that had happened only 80 or 100 years before. Indians are very particular in their relations of circumstances and events, and not half so apt to embellish as the whites, and the march of Soto through their country, and his fights with them, were affairs not likely to be forgotten by them, and would be handed down for a generation or two at least, very correct, no doubt. Even in my time, I have heard the old Indians, in their conversations, allude to the white warrior, or Tustanugga Hatke, as they called Soto.

You see I write, spell and dictate badly, but have given you what I heard from others who were best calculated to inform me upon such subjects. If there is anything in this that you have not seen or heard before, and you think it worth publishing, do so; if not, let it pass: for I assure you that I am not desirous to become conspicuous as a writer in a newspaper, or anything else—though I doubt much if the man lives that has seen as much of old Indian times, and heard as much of the early history of the Creeks, as I have. I would like to be where I could sit and tell it over to you; I could make you understand it much better.

May you live long and die rich.   T. S. W.

———

WHEELING, WINN PARISH, LA., } March 21, 1858. }

To J. J. HOOPER, ESQ.

Dear Sir—Some two weeks back I received the History of Alabama, sent me by my old friend "Horse Shoe Ned." It is a present made me by its Author—whom I have known from his childhood, and of course prize it highly, not only as a present from its author, but for the many new things to me that it contains. I should have commenced this sooner, but my son who resides near Hot Springs, Arkansas, and the only one of my family that is left me, has been with me for the last three weeks and has just left for his home. That, with my inability to

write at best, will make this not very interesting to you
or your readers.   What I write I dedicate to those that
read it.   You will see from what I write, and from what
I may write hereafter, that I differ from Col. PICKETT,
and what I write is not intended, nor can it detract in the
least from Col. PICKETT, as an author, a gentleman, or a
scholar.   I am not vain enough to think that I could
write anything like a history of any country (even if all I
should write were true) that would be interesting, while
Col. PICKETT is very capable of doing it ; he has not only
the advantages of a classical education, but was raised by
one of the most intelligent fathers in Alabama ; and as
to his mother, she has had her equals no doubt, but there
is no one living that can boast of a mother that was her
superior.   As to my own parents, I can say nothing more
than I recollect to have seen them and the only brother
I ever had, laid in their last resting place, within six miles
of where Savannah river takes its name.   My father died
in Franklin county, Georgia, near sixty years back ; my
brother about fifty-six years ; my mother about fifty-three
years back—leaving an only sister and myself, upon the
charity of the best world that I have seen, or any one
else, if they will take it right.   Now, sir, my whole history through life (though passing through some pretty
rough scenes by-the-by) would not be as interesting as the
lives of Washington and Marion, by Old Parson Weems ;
so I will close my own biography, and commence with
De Soto's march through Florida.
     Tampa Bay is the point, admitted by all, where Soto
(as I shall call him) debarked his men.   His army, composed of one thousand men, some on horseback and some
on foot, greyhounds as fleet as the wind, bloodhounds
large and ferocious, and in addition to all these, were lots
of Catholic priests, clergymen and monks.   This was
certainly a very imposing show, and was a show very well
calculated and no doubt did impose upon the unoffend-
ing natives, and the tons of iron, handcuffs, chains,
neckcollars and the like, were things well calculated to

inspire the natives with very exalted notions of the
Christianity they were soon to be taught.   No doubt but
that portion of the narrative is in a great measure true ; so
far as regards the true motives of those that set the
expedition on foot.   The object was gold or other plunder, and to diffuse among the natives a religion (as then
understood and practiced by those who were to propagate
it) that even had more laudable means been used to
establish it, would have benefited the Indians very little
more, if as much, as the worst pagan idolatry.   And it is
equally as shameful as true, that other Christian nations
have followed the example of Spain, with the natives of
this and other countries ; wherever the Bible (which was
seldom applied right) failed, the musket and bayonet were
resorted to.   The hogs and cattle are next : the introduction of those animals was the only philanthropic move-
ment during, or that attended, the expedition.   These
animals were landed as it appears, as early as May, 1539,
and Soto died between the last of May, 1542 and the 2d
July, 1543.   No date given of their leader's death, unless
we infer from the dates given in the narrative that he died
between the last of May, 1542, at which time he commenced the building of the brigantine, and the 1st of
June, 1542, which was the time his successor commenced
his march again in the wilderness, which was one day only
for commencing the work, for Soto to die, to be put in
the water, and his successor to march with the remainder
of the soldiers.   The portion of the history I have just
alluded to, you will find on pages 50 and 51, first volume.
Now had Col. PICCETT made a little blunder like this, I
should not have noticed it, for I know him to be much
clearer of committing such blunders than I can think myself to be, (I no doubt could prove that by you.) You will
find the day and month given in many places; but the
hero of the expedition dies, the day, month, or year is not
named.   I notice this to show that Portuguese and Spanish authors at all times are not to be relied on. Now,
sir, I have traveled through Florida, Georgia, Alabama,

Mississippi, Arkansas, and am pretty well acquainted with most of the neighborhoods that the history says Soto traveled through. Now, the idea of marching an army of a thousand men, making the marches as the history describes, and raising hogs, feeding on them, dividing them with the Indians, many left to be killed and packed up by the successor of Soto, and his men to feed on while at sea! Now, as this is a swine story, not written by St. Mark, I hope I may be at least permitted to doubt it, without sinning. There was the Christian Jean Ortez, who was a captive long enough to become so well acquainted with the language of the Florida Indians, which must have been the Yermacraws or flat-footed Yemassees, for they evidently were the first Indians that inhabited East Florida, the low parts of Georgia, and South Carolina, so far as we know; if not, then it must have been the Uchys, or Sowanokees, or Shawnese, for they were then nearest neighbors; we find this man Ortez interpreting, making speeches in Spanish, and in all the Indian dialects where De Soto passed. As I have lived longer among Indians than Ortez, and learned to speak so little, and it was not Sampson that killed the panther, I cannot be bound to believe that story, to be saved. Now, these same Portuguese and Spanish give us a description of the country they passed in the upper parts of Georgia and Alabama, and down to the waters of the Coosa. Now, every person that has read the history, and now knows the country, knows the account to be a highly exaggerated one. As to the Indian temples, I have nothing to say; every one that has seen an Indian town, has seen an Indian temple. That mode of traveling in a chair, carried by four men, differs from any traveling among them that I have seen or heard of. Those large barns of corn never fell to their lots in my time, or any of those old ones that I have been acquainted with, so far as I could learn; besides, the country, a few little creek valleys excepted, is a very poor one—that is, if you will examine the description given by those Portuguese and Spanish gentry, and then examine the country itself.

What I have wtitten is to show that the great probability is, that these writers have not been faithful in their narrations. For I have traveled more or less in and among all the tribes south of latitude 36 north, and some north of that line, between Georgia and Rio del Norte, and I think I am somewhat acquainted with the Indian character, and I am as certain of this as any one thing I never witnessed, viz: that De Soto, no other man, nor any set of men, could have reduced the Indians to such abject slavery. There is not one Indian, male or female, in one hundred, but would have put an end to their existence, rather than submit to such treatment. Even as late as 1836-7, I knew several Indian women who, rather than risk their children under the control of the Emigrating Indian Agent, put them to death, some of them large enough to walk; and these women had long been acquainted with the whites. In fact, I knew two men to kill themselves in Montgomery, rather than move, when their whole town people were along, and they not in any danger whatever. As long as ours has been a government, with so many tribes whose names have passed from the earth, there is not the mark of a pen, heiroglyphic, or any vestige whatever to show that such people ever were warmed by God's sun, I have never seen the first North American Indian slave, unless it was in Barbour county, Alabama. At what was known as the Pea River Fight, there were some Indian children taken prisoners, and they were mostly girls. I was in Barbour county as late as 1843. I there saw one or two of the children. If they have not been made slaves, I never have heard of any. The peons or foot soldiers in Mexico and the degraded Central American States are not looked upon, or at least by me, as North American Indians.. I have no doubt but the tribes inhabiting the tropical regions are much more submissive and timid than the hardy tribes inhabiting north and south of those regions. Besides, such gangs of priests, clergymen and monks, grey-hounds, blood-hounds, hand-cuffs, chains, neck-collars, (and such other holy material as De Soto introduced among the native Floridians, Georgians and Alabamians,) were too freely used for the same purpose among the Mexicans and Central Americans ; and the natives of those countries unfortunately lost their own language, and learned the language and embraced the religion of their oppressors, which has made them ten-fold worse than they were in their native state. You may take almost any other people that we read of and train them to be slaves, or at least make them perform those menial offices that slaves do ; but such is never the case with an Indian. It is true, you may, by kind treatment, either in word or action, get them occasionally to perform some little offices ; but harsh treatment, either in words or blows, never can control an Indian.

Now, after De Soto and his men had been rusticating in the country of the Coosas, they make their way to the Tallassees. They reach the town on the 18th September, 1540. De Soto remained at Tallassee twenty days, crossed over to the east side in canoes and on rafts, and traveled down the eastern side. Now, to show you how those Portuguese and Spaniards mistake things, Tallassee was always on the east side of the Tallapoosa, and Col. Pickett in a note of his own admits that Tuckabatchy was built on the opposite side, and all hands know that Tuckabatchy, Tookabatcha, was always on the west side. Now, there was no necessity for canoes and rafts after their stay of twenty days in Tallassee. Moreover, the river at that point is never past fording, only at a high stage of water. Besides, the season of the year in which De Soto was there, those who know the place will say to you that an Indian pony could ford it from Tallassee to King's Ferry, which is full three miles by water. The Tallassees and Tuckabatchy's were both original Musqua and Muscogees, and the oldest Indians and Indian countrymen that I have seen, say Tuckabatchy was settled years before Tallassee. I wrote you once before, that it was a long disputed point

with old Cusetaw and Tuckabatchee, which was settled
first, but that it was generally conceded that the Cusetaws
were the Spoakogees, or Spoakookulgees; that is, the
oldest settlers, or the mother of towns.

I know three men in Macon county who could have
given Col. Pickett Indian information of modern times,
(that is, for the last thirty years,) which is much more reliable than that he has had. I know something of the
settlement of the Tallassee town, opposite Tuckabatchy.
I will give you, some time before long, the history of the
settlement of Tallassee, and how that error crept into Col.
Pickett's History.

The three gentlemen alluded to above, in Macon county, are Nat. and John Callens and L. B. Strange.

I will here remark, that Col. Pickett's History has set
me right about the death of Alex. McGillivray. I had
thought he died as late as 1796, but find he died three
years before. His daughter and his last wife, who lived
by me for many years, could never tell; and if I ever
heard from others I forgot it.

I will in my next give you something of the Nitches,
Tallassees, and McGillivray's family.   T. S. W.

Wheeling, Winn Parish La.
March 25, 1858.

Eds. Mail:—I see in your paper of March the 11th that
"J. W. K." seems desirous to know if can give the origin
of the belief among the Chippewa Indians—and he pre-
sumes among others—that there is a deep gulf to be passed after death, before they can get to their Paradise. I
answer him candidly that I can not, and beg to be excus-
ed for my profound ignorance on the subject. In the first
place, the Chippewas are a people that I am as unac-
quainted with as I am of the gulf he speaks of. I have
heard of both, but have seen neither. I am satisfied that

such a people as the Chippewas do exist, for I have seen those that were said to have travelled among them, and I have seen and have travelled among several tribes of Indians—and for that reason I am satisfied that there is such a tribe as the Chippewas. As to the gulf, both the wicked that have fallen in and the good that have crossed it, are the same to us, as neither ever return to give us any information as to what is in the gulf or what there is beyond it. So, if these Indians have such a belief, they must have borrowed it from those that knew as little of such things as themselves. And even those that have instructed the Indians in their belief (if such there be) may have formed their religious notions either from fear, ignorance or interest—for, such has often been the case with those that pretend to much more than the native Indian. I have never heard of any such belief among those that I have been acquainted with; and those that I have conversed with upon religious subjects appeared to have correct notions of Deity—looked upon Him as an invisible being, who only made himself known to man through his works. J. W. K. says in this can be traced a likeness to the Christian belief. Whence came it? I answer, not from the Jews. Why, not believing the American Indian to be a descendant of the Jew proves nothing for or against the Christian religion. The gentleman says there is a marked resemblance in their laws with regard to marriages—that the children of Israel were not allowed to take wives among other nations, and such was the law among Indians. Such may have been the case—I will not dispute it. But, if such law ever existed, it was repealed long before my time; and if he will travel among them, and see the number of half-breeds of whites, negroes, and all others that have mixed, and will say that the law has not been repealed, I am certain that he will have the candor to admit that it has been grossly violated, at least. There may be something a little alike in the character of the Indian and the Jew. An Indian will sell the shirt off his back for whisky—the

Jew will his for money. The Indians, in their wars, often murdered men, women and children, and so did the Jews. By taking the 31st chap. Numbers, and perusing it closely, he will see that I am not mistaken as to the Jews. There was a custom in my time, among Indians, that there were many crimes punishable by their laws—and could the perpetrators of those crimes escape and lay out until their green-corn dance, and then reach the dance-ground undiscovered, they would go unpunished—but in no instance have I ever known murder to go unpunished, if the offender could be caught. The Wind family was allowed—and it was law that they should punish a murder at any and all times—but the other families were not allowed this privilege after a certain time.

As to the meeting of those versed in Indian history, I would like much to attend such a meeting; and if I am in possession of any information that others have not, I would most willingly impart it. Besides, nothing could afford me more pleasure than to meet at Montgomery. I should like to see it, now it is a city, as I knew it forty years ago a forest. But it is a pleasure, I fear, that my age and situation will deny me. Such a meeting, no doubt, would be interesting to many—bring up much of the past that has probably been forgotten, and be the means of explaining and doing away with many conflicting notions that have and do exist among various persons, in relation to Indians and their history, particularly those tribes that inhabited Alabama.

T. S. W.

WHEELING, WINN PARISH, LA.,
April 2, 1858.

F. A. RUTHERFORD, ESQ.

Dear Sir :—Your letter of the 8th ultimo, came to hand yesterday. You wish to know something of the early settlement and history of Macon and the adjoining counties. As to the history of the section of country you live in, I know much from 1813 to 1841, when I left Alabama. Many persons, who know what I do of the country and of the time I allude to, might write something that would interest you and some of your readers, but fear I shall not be able to do so. What I write, however, shall be *facts*, as well or better established than you generally get them, and perhaps some of them may be new to you and others.

From what I know of the Indians and their history, I think it as probable as anything that cannot be positively proven, that an occurrence in Macon county caused the Creek Indian war of 1813-'14. It was the murder of Arthur Lott, in 1812, by some Chetocchefaula Indians, a branch of the Tallasees. Lott was killed near what is known as the Warrior's Stand. He was moving to the then Mississippi Territory. His family moved on and settled at a bluff on Pearl River, which long went by the name of Lott's Bluff, but is now known as Columbia.

So soon as Col. Hawkins learned that Lott was murdered, he sent Christian Limbo, a German, to Cowetaw, to see Billy McIntosh, a half-breed chief. From Cowetaw, Limbo and McIntosh went to Thleacatska or Broken-arrow, to see Little Prince. The Prince was too old for active service, and sent a well known half breed, George Lovet, who was also a chief. Lovet took with him some Cussetas and McIntosh some Cowetas, and accompanied Limbo to Tuckabatchy to see the Big Warrior. He placed some Tuckabatchys under a chief called Emutta and the celebrated John McQueen, a negro, and all under the control of McIntosh, went in pursuit of the murderers. They found them on the Notasulga creek, at a place known since as Williamson Ferrell's settlement: where they shot the leaders and returned to their respective towns. This act aroused the Tallassees, and James McQueen, who had controlled them for 95 years having died the year before, his influence was lost, and from talks made some time before by Tecumseh the Sowanaka or Shawnee, and Seekaboo, a Warpicanata chief and prophet, (who was afterwards at the destruction of Ft. Mimms,) a number of the young warriors and a few old ones had become restless. Not long after Lott was killed, an old gentleman named Merideth was killed at the crossing on Catoma Creek, in what is now Montgomery county. This was done by the Otisees, in a drunken spree. The Big Warrior undertook to have them punished, but failed to do so, and in attempting to arrest them an Otisee was killed. A few days after this, the Otisees attacked a party of Tuckabachys, under the chief Emutta, at the Old Agency or Polecat Springs, which was then occupied by Nimrod Doyle. Doyle had been a soldier under Gen. St. Clair, was at his defeat and afterwards with Gen. Wayne.

About this time, or a little after, a chief, Tustanuggachee or Little Warrior, and a Coowersortda Indian, known as Capt. Isaacs, who had gone north-west with Tecumseh, were returning to the Creek nation, and learned from some Chickasaws that the Creeks had gone to war. Relying on this information, the Littte Warrior's party did some mischief on the frontier of Tennessee as well as killed a few persons. On their return to the nation they found that war had not actually broken out, but only the few little depredations that I have mentioned, had been committed. The Coowersortda Indians, Capt. Sam. Isaacs, (a name that he borrowed from an old trader who died some years back in Lincoln county, Tenn., and who was one of the most cunning, artful scamps I ever saw among the Indians,) gave the Big Warrior information about the murders in Tennessee. Isaacs from his tricks and management and having Alexander McGillvray's daughter for a wife, was let out of the scrape; but the Little Warrior being a Hickory-Ground Indian, set the Coosa Indians at variance with the Big Warrior. After this the Tuckabatchys, Ninny-pask-ulgees, or Road Indians, the Chunnanuggees and Conaligas all forted in, at Tuckabatchy, to defend themselves from those that had turned hostile.

I have often heard Sam Moniac say, that if Lott had not been killed at the time he was, it was his belief that the war could have been prevented. He and Billy Weatherfor have often said to me as well as others, that the Big Warrior at the time Tecumseh made his *talk* at Tuckabatchy, was inclined to take the talk, and at heart, was as hostile as any, if he had not been a coward. I have no doubt, from what I have heard Weatherford say, he (W.) was as much opposed to that war as any one living: but when it became necessary to take sides, he went with his countrymen, and gave me his reasons for so doing. He said, to join the whites was a thing he did not think right, and had it been so they would not have thanked him, and would have attributed it to cowardice. Besides, he said to remain with his people, he could prevent his misguided countrymen from committing many depredations that they might otherwise do. Weatherford was never a chief, though exercising as much or more influence over a part of the nation than many that were chiefs. He did not act the part which some writers say he did in the war, though I think he was fully as great a man as any have made him out to be. He was of a different order of man to what has generally been believed. As I knew him well and have had as good opportunities to become acquainted with his history and character, as most men that now live, I will, when I have leisure, give you Gen. Jackson and Col. Hawkins' opinion of the man, and what I think to be a more correct history than anything

3

I have seen written about him : and should any one doubt my judgment about him, none that knew these men *will* doubt theirs.

I left the Tuckabachys forted in, on the Tallapoosa. The Cowetaws, Cussetaws, Thleacatskas, Uchees, Oswich ees, Hitchetas and the Lower Eufowlas, under McIntosh, Joe Marshall, Timpoochy Barnard and some other Chattahoochee chiefs, went to their assistance. There was some skirmishing, though but little damage done on either side, and the Tuckabachys were carried to the Chattahoochee and Flint rivers, where they remained untill Gen. Floyd came into the nation.

I will close this by giving you the names of some few persons who have died and whose remains rest in Macon county. The first, is Gen. John Sevier, of Revolutionary memory. He rests at Ft. Decatur hill. James McQueen, who died, from all accounts, at the age of 128 years. He lived in the Nation 95 years, and was buried on the west bank of Naufapba creek. Just above Franklin, in the old field near Floyd's battle ground on Caleebee, rests James McGirth. He erected the first distillery in Alabama. James Connells, a noted half-breed, and the brother of McGillvray's last wife, sleeps by his side. Capt. Sam'l Butts was killed in the battle, and was buried on the ground; as were also Littleton Picket, Green Berry, John Thornton and many others. Capt. Wm. Owens, the father of Hardeman Owens, was buried at Ft. Hull. The Drummer, Dan'l Smith, that your father knew about Saundersville, Ga., more than fifty years ago, and Tom Blanks, a mess-mate of mine, sleep at the same place. Whitmael Williams, David Conyers and Leven Grear, from Washington county, Ga., were buried at what was once known as Fisher's old field, near the mouth of Caleebee. They were killed at Otisee. Capt. Arnold Seale, who lives in your neighborhood, was along at the time, and can tell you as much or more than I can write.

I will at some time try and send you an account of the settlement of Macon county, by many of its present citizens.

Yours, &c.,

T. S. W.

WHEELING, WINN PARISH, LA., } April 25th, 1858. }

COL. ALBERT J. PICKETT.

Dear Sir :—Your letter of the 23d February last, addressed to me through the Montgomery Mail, reached me some weeks since, and I have been too much engaged to write, had I been able to write anything worth reading, or to answer your inquiry about the Uchees and their language. All I can say about them is, that they occupied portions of Alabama, Georgia, and perhaps South Carolina. When the Creeks first settled the country, they were the neighbors of the Sowanoka or Shawnees, the Yemacraws, Yemasees and Hitchetas; though they in habits, customs and language were more like the Shawnees than either of the other three tribes I have mentioned. As to that guttural sound, or indescribable pronunciation of words, you are as able to account for it as I am. That guttural pronunciation was not alone confined to the Uchees; it seems to have been peculiar to those tribes that inhabited Alabama, Georgia and the Carolinas. Before the Muscogees settled Alabama and Georgia, from what I recollect of the Catawbas, Apilashs, Cherokees and Shawnees, they all more or less have that singular articulation, though not to so great an extent as the Uchees. It is yet noticeable among the common Cherokees and Shawnees; in fact the Uchees and Shawnees once could understand each other's language about as the Choctaws and Chickasaws do theirs. The Uchees were, like many other little tribes, broken up by the Creeks and those western bands that were connected with them. The Cherokees and Sowanokas were about all the tribes that the Crieks did not subdue. These two tribes were always able to stand their hands with the Muscogees, particular-the Sowanokas, until the whites began to encroach on them from the east. The tribe was then strong, and emigrated to the north-west. Many of the Uchees went north-west with the Shawnees. Those Uchees that remained in the country were allowed their own town Chiefs and a head Chief of their tribe, but were all under the general government of the Muscogees. The Uchees contended as long as they lived in the country that they could, man to man, whip the Creeks. And in Gen. Floyd's night fight, their leader, Timpoochy Barnard, fought much better than the friendly Creeks. With equal numbers teey could beat the Creeks at a ball play, for I have seen them do it often.

If the Uchees and Shawnees were not originally the same people, they had lived so long and so near each other as to become pretty well acquainted with each other's language. Many years ago I became acquainted with a Shawnee Chief in Texas, who headed a little band of his people that emigrated to that country very shortly after Gen. Harrison defeated them at Tippecanoe. This Chief spoke pretty good English—was very intellingent for an Indian—and was in the Tippecanoe fight, and has often related to me the particulars of that affair, or at least as he understood them. This man has, perhaps, been better known than almost any other Chief of any tribe in the early settlements of Texas and Arkansas. He remained in Texas until the American population commenced putting aside Spanish and Mexican customs. He then moved his people into a thinly settled portion of Arkansas. In 1841, a Mr. James Woodland and myself were travellng in Arkansas, and met with the Chief Spy Buck, (for that was his name.) I recollected to have seen or known him in Texas. He made many inquiries about me, and where I lived. I informed him I was living in the Old Musqua Country, and that I intended settling on the Washita river, at a point that he seemed to know;

and in January, 1842, I settled at the place spoken of. A week after my arrival at the place, Spy Buck and his party, a few Cherokees, some Choctaws, one or two Chickasaws, and a Delaware, all made their appearance. The Shawnees with Spy Buck, remained some two years near me, and then left for the Kansas river, except his youngest brother; he remained with me four years, or two years after the others left. From these people I learned much of their history. They gave the same account of being forced back from the Savannah and the settlements of the Musqua, in Alabama and Georgia, as the Creeks themselves had given. I had some Uchee negroes that spoke the Uchee, Creek, and Hitcheta; they and the Shawnees, could understand much of each other in Uchee; and that is one reason for believing that the Sowanokas and Uchees were once pretty much the same people. Among the many things I learned from Spy Buck, was that he had hunted with Savannah Jack or Sowanoka Jack above the Cross Timbers on Red River, after Jack had gone West. I see you speak of Jack in your history of Alabama. And as I was acquainted with Jack himself, and have had his history from many that knew him well, and its being connected with the history of Alabama as well as the Uchee Indians, it may not be uninteresting to give a sketch of it here. As I have before stated, a number of the Uchees went North-West with the Shawnees, many years ago. And not long after they reached their new homes on the waters of the Ohio, they commenced their depredations on the frontier settlers of Virginia and Pennsylvania. In one of their scouts they captured a white boy on the frontier of Pennsylvania, by the name of John Hague. This boy Hague was raised to manhood among them, and proved to be as great a savage as any of them. He took an Uchee woman for a wife and raised a number of children; it was also said that Hague raised an illegitimate son by a white woman named Girthy or Girty, and called his named Simon Girty, after his mother. This boy was brought up about Detroit. It

was said that he and a man by the name of Wells contributed much to the defeat of Gen. St. Clair. This I
have learned from several white men who knew Girty and
were with Gen. St. Clair. I will give you the names of
four of them, as they were known to many in Alabama
and Georgia: Nimrod Doyle, Absalom Hall, John Cone,
and Bob Walton. Doyle and Walton were both wounded at the defeat. Hague, who had grown old, remained
in the country until Gen. Wayne put an end to the troubles in that quarter. So soon as this was done, Hague
came South with his Indian family bringing with him
some Uchees and Sowanokas, and settled them on Fawn
Creek, or what is now known as Line Creek, near its
mouth and on the Mongomery side of the Creek. Hague
died and was buried on a mound near where there was
once a little village, settled by the whites, called Augusta.
This I have learned from Doyle, Walton Sam. Moniac,
Billy Weatherford and many others. And Savannah
Jack was his youngest son by the Uchee woman. I do
not know that it would be slandering the illustrious
dead to say that Jack was the Marshal Ney of the old
hostile Indians: Jack fought through the War, and after
their defeat at Horse Shoe, and Gen. Jackson moved his
troops to the place where he built Fort Jackson. The
Indians then became very much discouraged and commenced coming in. The chiefs who had controlled these
towns during the War would get in striking distance, to
hear what was to be done. Jack sent his women and
children out on the head waters of Catoma, and secreted
his warriors between a Cypress brake and the river, not
far above the present city of Monrgomery. Weatherford,
who was not a Chief, (but had more influence than many
that were,) placed his people on a little island in the Alabama river, near the mouth of Noland creek, that makes
into the river on the North or Autauga side, known as
Moniac's Island. Weatherford's people were Tuskegees.
Peter McQueen and his Talassees quartered themselves
upon the head waters of Line Creek. John and Sandy

Durant, the brothers of McQueen's wife, and also the brothers of Lochlin Durant, that you know, remained with McQueen. Josiah Francis, the Prophet, Nehe Marthla Micco, the Otisee chief, (both of them hanged, 1818, by Gen. Jackson,) placed their people not far above the Federal crossing on the Catoma. Hossa Yoholo, a very white half-breed chief, and the son of a man by the name of Powell, I think, took shelter in the dense cane forest in the bend opposite Montgomery. This man, from what I have learned, was one of the most reckless fighters in the nation. Ogillis Incha, or Menauway, who was the principal leader at Horse Shoe, and at the time was supposed to be killed, carried his people near the falls of Cahawba, where he remained for more than a year after peace was made.

This was the situation of those chiefs and their people about the time and shortly after General Jackson reached Franca Choka Chula, or the old French trading-house, as it was called by the Indians. Weatherford sent up old Tom Carr, or Tuskegee Emarthla, and he soon learned through Sam Moniac, his brother-in-law, (who was always friendly,) that he was in no danger, and so he came to camp, (but not in the way that it has been represented.) General Jackson, as if by intuition, seemed to know that Weatherford was no savage and much more than an ordinary man by nature, and treated him very kindly indeed. Savannah Jack, or, as he has been called by some, Sowanoka Jack, was not then as well known to the whites as many others. He frequented the camp pretty much unnoticed, (no doubt as he wished to be.) It was not long before it was understood that Jacksa Chula Harjo (as the Indians used to call Gen. Jackson,) wanted land to pay for the trouble he had been at, and that the Big Warrior and others were in favor of giving Old Mad Jackson, as they called him, as much land as he wanted. Jack—poor fellow—his little field happened to be on the Montgomery side of Line Creek, and of course would have to go with the ceded territory. This Jack could

not stand; he threatened to kill the Big Warrior and go
to fighting the whites again. It was soon understood
that a hostile chief was in camp, making threats, and the
General wished to see him; but Jack disappeared. He
took his warriors from the cypress brake near Montgomery, went out to Catoma, where his women and children
were, and there joined Francis and the Otisse chief.
Hossa Yoholo left the bend of the river at Montgomery
and joined Jack and his crowd, as also did McQueen and
the Durants. The boy, Billy Powell, who was the grand-
son of one of Peter McQueen's sisters, was then a little
boy, and was with this party. They all put out for Florida, and on their route they split among themselves.
Jack and his people being Uchees and Sowanokas, called
a halt on the Sepulga, about there and on the line of
West Florida, where he remained until he went West.
As to the history of his stay in that region, and what he
did before he left, you have already had it. I knew Capt.
Butler ánd the others he killed, and those who made
their escape. I knew Ogley—poor fellow! I staid one
night at his house in company with a Col. Turner Bynun,
of North Carolina, and his son, J. A. Bynum, who has
since represented the Halifax District, N. C., in Congress.
McQueen and the others went to East Florida. Sandy
Durant died at Tampa Bay, not long after they reached
the country. John Durant went to Nassau, on the Island
of New Providence. Peter McQueen remained in Florida until after Gen. Jackson's campaign of 1818, shortly
after which he died on a little barren island on the Atlantic side of Cape Florida. Hossa Yoholo, the white
half-breed chief, died on Indian river, in East Florida,
with a disease in his feet caused from an insect there
known as the jigger. This I learned from a hostile negro
who was raised with a family by the name of Powell, but
in after times was known as Holmes' Ned. He accompanied Hossa Yoholo or the Singing Sun to Florida. I
knew Ned many years: I purchased him from our friend,
Horse Shoe Ned, and he died mine.

I will here try and account to you for an error that
many have fallen into, about Billy Powell or Occola. As
I remarked before, this boy went with his uncle, McQueen,
to Florida. I knew him well after that, and have seen
him frequently. Capt. Isaac Brown and myself, with a
party of friendly Creeks and Uchees, made him a prisoner,
in 1818, and he was then but a lad. Capt. Brown is now
living in Bozier Parish, this State, and well recollects the
circumstance; for at the same time we captured Billy,
we re-captured a white woman that was made a prisoner
by the Indians at the massacre of Lieut. Scott and his
party, below the mouth of Flint river. She was then a
Mrs. Stuart, since a Mrs. Dill, of Fort Gaines, Ga. This
was at Osilla, and known as the McIntosh fight. This
boy having gone to Florida at the same time that Hossa
Yoholo went, then growing to be a man, and then being
called Ussa Yoholo, or Black Drink, after the killing of
Gen. Thompson, those that had heard of the fighter Hossa
Yoholo, of the old war, took Ussa Yoholo to be the same
man. You will see that the names, from the way they
are spelled, would sound pretty much alike, and they both
being Powells—but of different families—you can see how
the mistake could have easily orignated. Besides, I know
that Oceola, as he is called, was not a chief, nor ever was
known to the Tallassees as such, until after the killing of
Gen. Thompson.

You see that it is generally the half-breeds and mixed-
bloods that speak our language, that the whites get acquainted with; and if, in case of a little war or anything
of the sort, one of those that the whites know, go off
among the hostiles, he is by the whites dubbed a chief.
The Indians soon learn whom the whites look upon as being
their leaders, and not bing as ambitious of distinction as
the whites generally are, when any talking or compro-
mising is to be done, those persons are *put* forward.
Such was the case with Jim Henry and others, in 1836.
Jim Henry was never a chief in his life. His mother was
a Chehaw woman, and his father a Cuban Spaniard, and

one of those deserters from St. Augustine, Fla., long before
I knew anything about Indians. The father of Jim was
Antonio Rea. He once lived in Saundersville, Washington county, Ga., but that was before I knew him. A
Capt. McDougald took him to Fort Hawkins, from
whence he went to Chehaw, and thence to a place called
Pinder Town. One of the others was Emanuel, though
sometimes called Toney. He was the father of our Toney
that killed George Bonner, in 1836. The other was Tom
Peechin, known as Tom Pigeon. I saw an account, not
long since, of Joe Pigeon, a half-breed Choctaw, being
hanged in Mobile, for killing a cab-man. His mother
was no Choctaw; she was a Creek. Whenever you come
to know the truth, you will find that it was our Joe.
Old Tom, his father stopped at Pass Christian, and never
went with the Indians to Arkansas, as I have heard; besides killing a man for a few dollars was just suited to
Joe's morals. Although Joe's father was a Catholic, and
Joe a pupil of Mr. Compeer, his religious teachings did
him but little good. I knew him well, and he was certainly one of the worst half-breeds I ever knew.

When I commenced this, I had no idea of putting Joe
Pigeon in it; but he has passed up among other old acquaintances, and so I have to let him in. I will write
something else, next time.

Yours,

T. S. W

WHEELING, WINN PARISH, LA., }
June 13th, 1858.   }

J. J. HOOPER, ESQ.:

Dear Sir:—Some time in April last I directed a letter
to you which was intended to be addressed to Col. A. J.
Pickett, through you paper. Whether it reached you or
not I do not know; if it did, and has been published, I

would be glad to get the number of your paper that contains it, as I have promised a friend to let him have what I write to you and others, relative to Indian history, and the early settlement of Alabama. Your paper, until within the last two months came more regularly than any I take; since that time, I seldom see or hear of a Montgomery Mail. I do not recollect the last number of the Mail I did get. This country is like most others that I have lived in—too few reading people, and too many of that few find it more convenient to borrow a newspaper than pay for one; so I very often have mine loaned out. And that is why I cannot recollect the last number I received. But I recollect among the last numbers that I have seen, there was a sketch, I think, taken from a Boston paper, giving an account of the meeting of three Scotch brothers in Charleston, Mass., which meeting was not of very common occurrence; and, on reading that, I sketched off the meeting of two brothers, that I witnessed, many years ago, in what is now Alabama, but then was the Creek nation, and which I did not send to you.

Some years before the Creek war, and when I was quite a youngster, I made occasional vists to the Ocmulgee river, which was then the line between the whites and Indians. The Indians claimed half the river, and in spring or shad-catching time the Indians would flock from all parts of the nation in great numbers to the Ocmulgee. They could be seen at every shoal as high up the river as shad could run, down to the Altamaha, for the purpose of fishing. On one of my trips to Old Fort Hawkins, I became acquainted with an Indian countryman by the name of John Ward; and the first time I ever visited the Creek agency, which was then on Flint River, was in company with Ward, an old uncle of mine, and one Andrew McDougald. Col. Hawkins was then holding a council with some chiefs from various parts of the nation. I met with Ward occasionally from that time until the war commenced. When Gen. Floyd moved his troops to Flint River, Ward was the interpreter for the officer that

was in command at Fort Manning. He then came into
Gen. Floyd's camp, and remained with the army until it
reached the Chattahoochee, and commenced building
Fort Mitchell. He was often sent out with Nimrod Doyle
as a spy. There was also an Indian countryman along by
the name of Bob Moseley. Moseley's wife was the niece
of Peter McQueen. Ward's wife was a relation of Daniel
McDonald, more generally known to the whites as Daniel
McGillivray, and both of their wives were then with the
hostile Indians. Ward and Moseley seemed willing to
risk any and everything to forward the movements of the
army, in order to reach the neighborhood of their families.
There was a detachment of soldiers sent out to Uchee
creek, to throw up a breast-work. I was one of the party,
and among the rest was a Baptist preacher by the name
of Elisha Moseley, a very sensible and most excellent man
at that, and as brave as men ever get to be; for he could
pray all night and fight all day, or pray all day and fight
all night, just as it came to his turn to do either; and this
preacher was a brother to Bob Moseley, the Indian countryman. While at this breast-work, one night, by a camp-
fire, I listened to Elijah Moseley inquiring into his brother's motives for leaving a white family and making his
home among a tribe of savages. Bob's reply was, as well
as I now recollect, that there was no false swearing among
Indians. The preacher then commenced making some
enquiry into Ward's history. Ward informed him that
his father had taken him into the Creek nation near
where Oweatumka or Wetumpka now stands, when he
(Ward) was a child, and shortly after died, and that he
recollected very little of his father; that he had been
raised by Daniel McDonald, or McGillivray, as he was
commonly called; that he heard McDonald say that his
father was a Georgian, and had left a wife and children
in that State. Ward's history, as far as it went, soon became known in the camp; and some one in the camp,
that had heard of Ward's father quitting his family and
disappearing with one of his children, and knowing some-

tning of the Wards in Georgia, looked at John Ward and said, from the near resemblance of him and a Georgia Ward, they must be brothers. The Georgia brother was written to, and in a few weeks, made his appearance in camp. In this time, the Indian Ward, from exposure, had fallen sick, and was very low. The Georgia brother came into camp one night, and the next morning John Ward was a corpse—though John was perfect rational on the arrival of his brother and, before he died, knew who he was. They proved to be twin brothers. A very intimate acquaintance of yours messed with me at the time, and Ward frequently messed with us. It was Capt. Arnold Seals, of Macon county, Ala. Ward died in one of the tents of Adams' riflemen, and Elijah Moseley was his nurse. The most feeling pulpit talk I ever heard dropped from the lips of Elijah Mosely, in a soldier's tent, on the death of John Ward. Ward left one son. John, though raised among Indians, spoke our language very well. John's mother was a Tuskegee. He was entitled to a half section of land, under the treaty, and was enrolled among the Tuskegees. He was a floater, under the treaty, but by the permission of Col. Albert Nat. Collins, of Macon county, and myself, he located him a tract in the fork of Coosa and Tallapoosa. I think he sold to Col. George Taylor. The Indian countryman, John Ward, died in 1813. His remains rest on the hill just above old Fort Mitchell. So do the remains of two other Indian country-men—Tom Carr, an Englishman, and the father of Paddy Carr, and lame Bob Walton. Col. Hawkins used to call him Timor Bob, and said he was as brave, if not the bravest man he ever knew. He was the interpreter for Col. Hawkins, and accompanied him to the Hickory Ground, with Sam Moniac, Billy Weatherford, Pinthlo Yoholo, or Swamp Singer, and old Eufau Harjo, or Mad Dog, at the time he arrested Boles, the Englishman, at the head of fifteen hundred Indian warriors. If old Col. Joe Hutchinson is living, he can give you a full history of that affair; and if dead, a letter, in the hand writing of

Col. Hawkins, may be found among his papers, detailing the history of the whole matter. On the hill where rest the remains of these men I have mentioned, as well as many others that I could name, moulders the right arm of Lieut. Tennell. He was a gallant man—was wounded at Otissee. His arm was amputated by Dr. Charles Williamson, at Fort Mitchell. Those things are as fresh in my memory almost as when they occurred—at least, much more so than many things that have occurred long since.

I will close this by saying to you, that I wrote another letter to Col. Pickett, trying to prove to him that I was better acquainted with Indian history than himself; but not knowing whether the first was published, I decline sending it, thinking it probable that they were getting too long and uninteresting for publication; and, from my manner of writing, I could give no satisfaction—if satisfaction I could give at all—and have them much shorter.

I hope my old Tar River friend, Horse Shoe Ned, still lives and enjoys good health. I would give more to see him and Lewis Tyus than I would to read all the speeches that have been spoken and all the letters that have been written on Kansas affairs.

Yours,
T. S. W.

———

From the Columbus (Ga.) Sun.

Eds. Sun: In the spring of 1818, the writer was in Gen. Jackson's army, in Florida, consisting of near 4,000 men, including regulars commanded by Gen. Gaines; Georgia militia commanded by Gen. Glascock; the Tennessee horsemen and friendly Indians under Gen. McIntosh. Major Thomas Woodward and Captain Isaac Brown had a kind of joint command with McIntosh over the Indians.

While marching on between St. Marks, and Sewannee Town, distance about one hundred miles, on Sunday, the

12th day of April, we discovered fresh signs of Indians. Gen. McIntosh, with his command of Creek Indians, pursued them. The main army, as was our habit, lay down in the grass to rest and await McIntosh's return. Very soon McIntosh overtook them, and the battle commenced in hearing of us, probably a mile off. We could hear the firing of guns, which continued for some time.

Well I remember an express borne from McIntosh. An Indian, on foot, running, crying out, at the top of his voice, "Captain Jackson, Captain Jackson." As he passed us, we pointed to Old Hickory, who soon dispatched a company of Tennessee mounted men to aid McIntosh. The battle was finished ere they reached him. McIntosh and Woodward soon returned to our camp with their prisoners, consisting of women and children, and a *white woman* to our surprise. This woman is still living in or about Fort Gaines. She was then Mrs. Stuart, and afterwards married John Dill, of Fort Gaines, who died a few years since.

For the particulars of her capture by the Indians and re-capture by McIntosh and Woodward, I refer you to the enclosed letter, which I have just received from Gen. Woodward, which, if you think of sufficient interest, please copy in full, or make such extracts as you choose. Since receiving this letter from Gen. Woodward I have hunted up my diary, kept during that campaign, and have made the above extracts.   B.

WHEELING, WINN PARISH, LA., }
June 16th, 1858. }

COL. JOHN BANKS:

Dear Sir: Your letter of the 27th ult. is as welcome as it was unexpected. Anything from those I knew in early life is consoling to my feelings in my present lonely situation, particularly when it contains such kindly expressed feelings for my welfare here and my happiness hereafter. In your P. S. you say I may have forgotten you. Your name is a familiar one to me, and it is possi-

ble I may not know which one of that name I am writing
to, but it would be treating unkindly one of the best
memories that man ever had to doubt it.   If you are the
John Banks I think I am writing to, you were born
in Georgia, and in the same county I was, Elbert.

In 1818 there were two companies of soldiers from
Elbert county, Ga., one commanded by Capt. Mann; the
other by Capt. Ashley.   You were a Lieutenant in one
of them.   I remember the trip to Fort Early that you
speak of, as I do most of what occurred in that Florida
expedition.   That was a little over forty years ago.   The
names you mention in your letter are as familiar to me
as my own.   The two women whose names you mention,
if the incidents connected with their lives were as well
known to some as they are to myself, would afford material for a very interesting book.   Mrs. Stuart (now Mrs.
Dill) you saw when Capt. Brown and myself carried her
to your camp; you know something of her history—at
least you know something of her being a captive among
the hostile Indians.   And as I have nothing to do to-day,
and you live in Columbus among many of my old acquaintances as well as relatives, and perhaps some of
them would be willing to hear that I am living at least, I
will give you a little of their (Mrs. Dill's and Mrs. Brown's)
history.

In 1816 and 1817, the Florida Indians were doing mischief, and the Government found it necessary to keep
troops quartered on the borders of Florida.   Fort Scott
and Fort Huse were erected to protect the settlers in
Early county, Georgia.   That was then a new and thinly
settled country.   The command of the troops was given
to Colonel Arbuckle.   He had frequent skirmishes with
the Indians, under the control of Chitto-Fanna-Chula, or
old Snake Bone, but known to you and the whites generally as old Ne-he-mathla.   The present gallant General
Twiggs was then a Brevet Major in the 7th Regiment of
Infanty, and was generally the foremost in those skirmishes.   Supplies for the troops had to be carried from

New Orleans and Mobile by water. A very large boat with army stores was started from Mobile Point under the command of Lieut. Scott. Mrs. Stuart was among those on board; her husband, a Sergeant, and a fine looking man at that, had gone with the troops by land. The boat, having to be propelled by oars and poles, was long on the trip, and by this time the war had completely opened. The old hostile Creeks, from various portions of Florida, were engaged in it; among others the two Chiefs you saw hanged at St. Mark's—Josiah Francis and Ne-he-mathla Micco. They headed a party and watched the boats. As those on board were hooking and jamming (as the boatmen called it) near the bank, and opposite a thick canebrake, the Indians fired on them, killing and wounding most of those on board at the first fire. Those not disabled from the first fire of the Indians made the best fight they could, but all on board were killed except Mrs. Stuart and two soldiers—Gray, and another man whose name I have forgot, if I ever knew it; they were both shot, but made their escape by swimming to the opposite shore. I must here mention a circumstance that occurred on board the boat at the time, which I learned from one of the men who escaped, and also from some of the Indians who were present. There was a Sergeant named McIntosh, a Scotchman, on board, whom I knew well. He was with Colonel, afterwards General Thomas A. Smith, before St. Augustine, Fla., in 1812, and a Sergeant in Capt. Woodruff's company, at the beginning of the war of 1812, and was a favorite among officers and soldiers. He was an own cousin of the Indian General McIntosh you knew, whose grave you say you not long since visited. Sergeant McIntosh was a man of giant size, and perhaps more bodily strength than any man I have known in our service. When he found all on the boat were lost, and nothing more could be done, he went into a little kind of cabin that the Lieutenant had occupied as his quarters, in which was a swivel or small cannon; loaded it, took it on deck, and resting the

4

swivel on one arm ranged it as well as he could, and (the Indians by this time were boarding the boat) with a fire-brand, he set off the swivel, which cleared the boat for a few minutes of Indians. At the firing of the swivel he was thrown overboard and drowned, and this clearing of the Indians from the boat for a short time gave Gray a chance to escape. Mrs. Stuart was taken almost lifeless as well as senseless, and was a captive until the day I carried her to your camp. After taking her from the boat, they (the Indians) differed among themselves as to whose slave or servant she should be. An Indian by the name of Yellow Hair said he had many years before been sick at or near St. Mary's, and that he felt it a duty to take the woman and treat her kindly, as he was treated so by a white woman when he was among the whites. The matter was left to an old Indian by the name of Bear Head, who decided in favor of Yellow Hair. I was told by the Indians that Yellow Hair treated her with great kindness and respect. I never asked her any questions as to her treatment, and presume she never knew me from any other Indian, as Brown and myself were both dressed like Indians. We knew long before we re-captured her what band she was with, and had tried to come up with them before.

The most tiresome march I ever made was one night in company with the present Gen. Twiggs. He with some soldiers, and I with a party of Indians, trying to rescue her at old Tallahassee, but the Indians had left before we reached the place. I shall never, while I live, forget the day we took her from the Indians. Billy Mitchell, a son of the then Indian agent, Brown, Kendall Lewis, John Winslett, Sam. Hall and myself, were the only white men that were with the Indians, except old Jack Carter, my pack-horseman. The white men I have named and the Hitchetas under Noble Kenard, and the Uchees under Timpoochy Barnard, commenced the fight. Shortly after the firing commenced, we could hear a female voice in the English language calling for help, but she was concealed from our view. The hostile Indians, though greatly inferior in number to our whole force, had the advantage of the ground, it being a dense thicket, and kept the party that first attacked at bay until Gen. McIntosh arrived with the main force. McIntosh, though raised among savages, was a General; yes, he was one of God's make of Generals. I could hear his voice above the din of fire-arms— "Save the white woman! save the Indian women and children!" All this time Mrs. Stuart was between the fires of the combatants. McIntosh said to me, "Chulatarla Emathla, you, Brown and Mitchell, go to that woman." (Chulatarla Emathla was the name I was known by among the Indians.) Mitchell was a good soldier and a bad cripple from rheumatism. He dismounted from his horse and said, "Boys, let me lead the way." We made the charge with some Uchees and Creeks, but Mitchell, poor fellow, was soon left behind, in consequence of his inability to travel on foot. I can see her now, squatted in the saw-palmetto, among a few dwarf cabbage trees, surrounded by a group of Indian women. There I saw Brown kill an Indian, and I got my rifle-stock shot off just back of the lock. Old Jack Carter came up with my horse shortly after we cut off the woman from the warriors. I got his musket and used it until the fight ended. You saw her (Mrs. Stuart) when she reached the camp, and recollect her appearance better than I can describe it.

You say you have seen the old lady, the mother of Isaac Brown. I never saw her but once, and that was in Twiggs county, Ga., about the last of February, 1818. It was at her own house. I called there to get Isaac to go with me into Florida, as I had been ordered by General Jackson to collect as many Indians as I could and join him at Fort Scott. Isaac had no horse that was suitable for the trip. I left my horse with Gen. Wimberly, and we took it on foot to Fort Early, trusting to Providence for horses after that. When we were about to leave, the old lady said, "Isaac, my son, the Indians killed your fa-

ther, and may kill you, but I had rather hear of your being killed than to hear that my son had acted the coward."
This is all the acquaince I ever had with the old lady;
but I have had her history from many that knew her
well. When Isaac was an infant, his father, who was a
fearless man, crossed the Oconee river near what is known
as the Long Bluff. The Oconee was then the line between the whites and Indians. Brown built him a house,
and was preparing for stock raising. He always kept on
hand a number of loaded guns and some fine dogs. One
morning about daylight his dogs commenced barking;
he opened the door to look out and was shot dead by an
Indian, who had secreted himself near the house. At the
report of the gun, the Indians raised the yell. Mrs.
Brown drew her lifeless husband into the house, shut the
door, and commenced firing at the Indians, and succeeded
in driving them off. They soon returned, and set fire to
a board shelter attached to the house. She climbed up
the wall on the inside; and with a basin of milk extin-
guished the fire; and while in the act of pouring the
milk on the fire, with her arm projecting through the
logs, the Indians shot at and broke her shoulder. With one
arm and the aid of a small boy, the son of one James
Harrison, she succeeded the second time in driving the
Indians away. She then escaped across the river with
her children. A company was collected and repaired to
the house, and they said it had not been a sham fight,
for they found the white man in the house shot dead, and
not far from the house two dead Indians, and not far
from their trail were discovered signs as though they had
been dressing wounds. Now you can account for Isaac
Brown's being a soldier as easily as to account for Lexington and his half-brother, Lecompte, being race horses
—it's in the blood. The boy that was with Mrs. Brown,
was the son of James Harrison, who was a man of great
daring and had suffered much from the Indians, and they
in return had suffered much from him. He was the man
who killed the father of the present speaker of the Creeks,

Hopothleyoholo, and was known to the Indians as Epha
Tustanugga, or Dog Warrior, and to the whites as Davy
or David Cornels. Davy Cornels, I suspect, was the cause
of more mischief done to the whites by the Creek Indians
than any man that ever lived in the nation. He was
troublesome during the Revolution and long after. While
Seagroves was agent, Cornels sent him word that he
wished to be at peace, and would meet him at Colerain,
not a great way from St. Mary's. Seagroves unfortunately let it be known that he was expecting a visit from
Cornels. Harrison heard of it, collected a few men, and
I suspect Brown's father among the rest. All had suffered
long and much from the depredations of Cornels and his
men; they knew his path; they watched it closely, and
one day as he approached them with a white flag, Harrison
killed him. So ended the life of the most bitter enemy
the whites ever had among the Creek Indians, Sowanoka
Jack excepted.

By the time you get through what I have here scribbled, I reckon you will be a little cautious how you write
to your old Indian acquaintances who have little else to do
than sit and think over old times. You say you reckon I
am now an old man; you are right. Time, the common
leveler of our race, has not passed me unnoticed, and according to the course of things it will not be a great while
before I am turned over to the terror of kings. If you
see Jack or Thacker Howard, tell them I am living. May
you live as long as suits your convenience.

Respectfully,

T. S. W.

WHEELING, WINN PARISH, LA., }
June 21st, 1858. }

COL. A. J. PICKETT:

Dear Sir:—I addressed to you, in April last, a letter
through the Montgomery Mail. Some few days after I
forwarded that, I wrote a second one, which I intended
for you, but not knowing that my first was published, I
declined sending the second. But a few days back I received the number of the Mail in which my letter was
published. Whether you found that either instructive or
interesting, I cannot say; but inasmuch as that has been
published I shall risk another, and if our friend Hooper
finds it too long and uninteresting, he can do with it as
he has to do with other trash—throw it aside, or commit
it to the flames.

In you letter to me of February last, you mentioned
something of the inquiry I made in a private letter to my
friend Hanrick, about a manuscript. Why that inquiry
was made, I had learned that you had had, at one time,
the manuscripts of George Stiggins, and possibly I might
learn something of the manuscript I loaned him. I had
no idea that anything I had written would be used by
you, or any one else, in the history of a country; but the
manuscript of Christian Limbo, taken from Col. Hawkins'
writings, I would have been glad to have gotten hold of, as
it contained much I think (if now published) that would be
new to you and others, and entertaining to all who take an
interest in Indian history. Besides, it contained the
copies of two letters written as far back as 1735, by Sir.
James or Gen. Oglethorpe. They were written at different times, but both written at Frederica, on St. Simond's
Island. The letters were directed to James McQueen,
requesting him to use his influence with the Indians and
prevent them, if possible, from taking sides with the

Spaniards who were then threatening to attack the infant
colony of Georgia. The letters were written in a style
very different from letters written at the present day; and
the bearer of those letters was a Scotchman named Malcolm McPherson. He was the natural father of Schoya,
or Seboy McPherson, and she was the mother of Davy
Tate and Billy Weatherford, and was not the daughter of
Lauchlan McGillivray, as has been represented. Mc-
Pherson was the man that gave Lauchlan McGillivray
his first start as a trader. McGillivray came to the Creek
nation in company with John Tate and Daniel McDonald.
John Tate was the father of Davy Tate, and was the last
agent the English Government ever had among the
Creeks. During the American revolution, Tate raised a
large number of Indians on the waters of Alabama, and
from almost every town (except the Tallassees and Net-
chez, who, through the influence of McQueen, never did
take up arms against the colonies during the revolution.)
Tate carried his warriors to Chattahoochee, and there
joined Tusta Nuggy Hopoy, or Little Prince, with the
Chattahoochee Indians, and started to Augusta, Ga., to
aid a Col. Grierson, better known as Grayson, a Tory
Colonel. Near the head springs of the Upatoy creek, and
near old Fort Perry, Tate became deranged; the cause I
never learned. He was brought back to old Cussetaw
and died; he was buried on a high hill east of the old
town, and near what was the residence of Gen. Woolfolk
when I left the country. I have been shown his grave
often, and have heard what I have stated from Little
Prince, and a hundred others that were along at the time.
When Tate died, the Alabama Indians mostly returned,
except the Tuckabatchys under Efau Tustanuggy, or Dog
Warrior. (He was known to the whites as Davy Cornels;
he was the father of the present speaker of the Creeks,
Hopoithleyohola, and a brother of Alexander McGillivray's
last wife.) This man with his warriors accompanied the
Little Prince and his party to Augusta, and did some
fighting and much other mischief.

This man Davy Cornels did more mischief to the whites than any man that has lived among the Creeks, and was the most hostile and bitter enemy the whites ever had among the Creeks, Savannah Jack excepted. While Seagrove was agent, Cornels sent him word he wished to be at peace and would visit him at Colerain, near St. Mary's. It was known to some whites that Seagrove was expecting a visit from Davy Cornels—a James Harrison that had suffered much by the Indians, way-laid Cornels' path and killed him, bearing a white flag. We might go back to Lauchlan McGillivray; he was a Scotch-man, as was Tate. And not long before or after Tate had left the nation for Augusta, McGillivray took his two children, Sophy and Alexander, and started for Savannah; the Americans lay around Col. Campbell's camp or fort in such numbers that he was forced to send his children back to the nation by his negro man Charles. Charles lived with and about me for years, and I have heard him and others who corroborated his statement, tell it often. Sophy was the oldest of the two. So, you see, you and I differ widely as to the time Alexander McGillivray came into existence, because Alex. McGillivray's mother was not the dauther of a Frenchman or French officer. She was a full blooded Tuskegee Indian. Your history says Alexander was the first born of Lauchlan McGillivray and Sehoy Marchand. I speak nothing but the truth-when I tell you that I know my oportunities for informa, tion on tuis subject have been much better than yours, and that Sophy was the oldest child and an own sister to Alexander, and that will do away with the dream of so much books and papers. Your history says that the mother of Tate and Weatherford was a sister to Alexan-der McGillivray. I will now tell you how you have been led into that error; I see you speak of the Wind tribe of Indians, and I also see that you give Barrent Deboys' versions of it; he never could tell the difference between clan as family and a tribe. I have before this, in one of my letters to Mr. Hooper, tried to explain this family arrangement. The Creek Indians were laid off in families or clans, as were the Scots with their Campbells, McPhersons, McGregers, and so on, with this difference: the Scotch clans had just as many privileges as their numbers and the strength of their arms would allow them. The privileges of the Indian clans were prescribed by their laws, but the Wind family or clan were always allowed more than the Bears, Panthers, Foxes and others; and any of these families in speaking of the family to which he or she belonged, claimed kin with the whole family as brother, sister, uncle, aunt, and at the same time be noways related by blood. And as to what family Tate and McGillivray's wives belonged, I do not pretend to say, though I am certain that's the way the relationship has come about. For I never heard of the mother of McGillivray being crossed upon the French until I saw it in your history. But always understood her to be a full Indian, and the mother of Tate and Weatherford to be a half-breed, and the most interesting woman in the nation of her time.

I see in your history, for the first time I ever heard of such a thing, that Alexander McGillivray was an educated man. That's new to me as it would have been to himself, could he have been shown it in his day. The letters purporting to have been written by him which appear in the History of Alabama, are well written, and show conclusively that they emanated from no ordinary man. But could the author of those letters and McGillivray to whom they are ascribed, look back, they could say that the world is yet as credulous as in their time. If there is any one living that can or could identify the hand writing of a Scotchman by the name of Alex. F. Leslie, he could easily tell who wrote those letters. This man Leslie did McGillivray's writing and was worthy of (so far as intellect is concerned) the notice of his distinguished relative of our own country, General Alexander Hamilton.

Leslie was by birth a Scotchman. He came to the

Island of Barbadoes when a young man; from thence
to St. Augustine, Fla. He was engaged in business
with Forbes, Panthou and others; spent much of his
time among the Creek Indians; and was the father of
the half-breed Alexander Leslie that the Fort of Talladega was called after. That was Fort Leslie and not
Fort Lashly, as they have given it to you. This much,
I knew the half-breed as well as any other in the Nation. The history of his father I have had from Hamby
and Irish Doyle, (not Nimrod Doyle,) both well educated men, and in the service of Panthon, Forbes and Leslie for years; besides, I heard Gov. McIntosh, of Florida, many years ago, speaking of the many shrewd men
that had at an early day come to Florida, say that this
man Leslie was the most talented man of the whole.
I knew Gov. Clark, of Ga., Gen. Adams, Col. Sam.
Alexander and (not James Alexander) all Indian fighters and frontiermen—knew McGillivray well—and all
spoke of him and admitted him to be a man of great
natural sense, but never learned from any of them that
he was an educated man.

I knew Gen. Newnan well—served with him long in
the army. He was an officer at Fort Wilkinson when
the meeting you speak of took place between General
Pickens and others with McGillivray, at the Rock Landing. Gen. Newnan knew both the men, and said Billy
McIntosh was the greatest man of the two—that is,
McIntosh and McGillivray. Now, for a moment, if your
history of that meeting be correct, and no doubt it is,
it will prove that McGillivray was not the man of learning that you represent him to be. His quitting the
Council, going off to the Ocmulgee with his people,
writing back that he left to get a good feeding ground
for his horses—I know every foot of ground and every
branch he crossed, and through what is now Baldwin
and Jones counties, was then one of the best range
countries that ever existed in Georgia or Alabama.
That portion of your history gives the true character of

McGillivray, as it does the true character of the Indian when a talk don't suit them; break up and go off. But it was a subterfuge that so able and learned a man, so superior to those commissioners on the part of United States diplomacy, would not likely have resorted to. To detract or hide, willfully, from the world what the dead merited while living, would be unpardonable, but every thing that is said or written of those departed ones, (or even living ones,) to make them greater than they really were, that much the biographer does at his own expense. I never knew McGillivray, but I think I know his true character as well as any now living, and better than many that knew him when living, as I have mingled much with both whites and Indians that knew him well. As I once wrote to a gentleman before I ever saw your history, had Alexander McGillivray been living in the War of 1813 and '14, and could have united his people, the history of that war would have been a very different one to what it is. I know it was the opinion of Gen. Washington that McGillivray acted with duplicity towards our government, and you in your history give the reader to think that he was a treacherous man. But I differ with your history as I do with the best man that has left his name on record, as to McGillivray's true character. I know that McGillivray never liked our people or our government, but that he carried out every promise that he ever made, and in good faith too, I have no doubt. I have learned this from those that knew him—knew his feelings, and the awkward situation he was placed in, and what he had contended with. He had to deal more or less with the United States, England, and Spain, all three jealous of McGillivray, and all jealous of each other; it would have taken a man North of Mason and Dixon's line to wear a face to have suited all those that McGillivray had to deal with and make any thing of a fair show.

Another thing that satisfies me McGillivray was not the learned man, or man of letters, that you make him to be ; you can find no letters from Gen. Washington to him, or from him to Gen. Washington ; perhaps a letter or two to Gen. Knox, written by Leslie, with McGillivray's name attached to them, may be found, but no others. The idea of McGillivray, (with the learning you give him,) suffering himself dubbed General, in a government where the organic law of the land prohibited his being a citizen, is as absurd as any thing can be. And then trapsing the streets of cities with an American uniform on, is suited to the Indian character, but not that of a profound scholar. Besides, I am very much inclined to doubt if there is a record in existence to show or prove that he ever mastered the Latin and Greek languages, in any school either in South Carolina or Georgia, and am as much inclined to doubt their being a Masonic Lodge or Chapter that can show that he was ever a member of one or both. I was raised in Georgia, but have never read its history, nor have I ever heard before I saw it in your history, of those large confiscated estates of Lauchlan McGillivray. Though I have often heard that Malcom McPherson and George Galpin lost much by the war and the British, but not by the Americans. I knew Davy Tate well and spent near seven weeks with him at one time, many years ago ; he was decidedly the most sensible and well informed man I have ever seen of the Indian blood, (that is the Creek ;) he was not educated; a man of much truth, and like his half-brother, a man of great firmness. He has talked to me much ; I never heard him say that McGillivray was a man of letters. But he has often said to me that MbGillivray lived pretty much upon the property of his (Tate's) father, and that the man Daniel McDonald, that I have before spoken of who came to the country with Lauchlan McGillivray and John Tate, that after the disappearance of Lauchlan McGillivray from the country, he (Daniel McDonald) assumed the name of Daniel McGillivray, and fell heir to most of McGillivray's property that he left in the nation. This I have learned from others, as well as Davy Tate.

This man Daniel McDonald, or Daniel McGillivray, was the father of the chief known as Bit Nose Billy Mc-Gillivray. The Gen. Leclerk Milfort you frequently refer to as authority, I never heard of, though I have often heard of a little Frenchman by the name of Milfort Dusong, who had lived in the nation before I knew it; this man Milfort had an Indian wife and left one son, Alexander or Sandy Dusong. I knew him; he emigrated with the Creeks to Arkansas in '36 and '37· It is not unfrequently the case with Indians, as it is with the whites, to claim relationship with distinguished persons, particularly Virginians. I have not seen a little darkskined, swarthy man from Virginia, for the last thirty years, no matter what race he sprang from, but claimed kin with John Randolph, and the Powetan family.

I knew Alexander McGillivray's children well; his daughter Peggy was the wife of Charles Cornels, and died before Cornels hung himself. His daughter Lizzy lived by me for years; I purchased hers and her son's land. They were located on section 16, in township 16 and range 24; it lies in Macon county, near Tuskegee; I sold it to James Dent. I lived many years by Mrs. Mc-Girth; she was McGillivray's last wife; spoke good English,—from none of these did I ever learn that he was a scholar.

I could say much more upon this subject, but this is already too long. I will close this by saying to you, that as you and I both have had to rely upon the statements of others for what we write, and you much more than myself, we will remain as we always have been, friends, and let those that read what we write judge which is most likely to be right. When I have time I will write and point out many errors that you have been led into that I know of my own knowledge, and come within the knowledge of others that still live. It is our nature when we say or write a thing, to wish the world to believe us right, (and many wish it if they know they are wrong.) But there is nothing more noble and generous in a man,

than when he finds he is in error to own and abandon it.
And as there has been some little interest taken or felt in
what I have written, if I can, I will spend a month or two
in Montgomery next winter. I could tell you many
things that have been forgotten, and could point out
many places that would interest you and others that are
living there.

Yours, &c.,
T. S. W.

———

WHEELING, WINN PARISH, LA. }
July 8, 1858. }

J. J. HOOPER, ESQ.:

Dear Sir: The entry of Gen. LaFayette into Alabama,
was the most imposing show I witnessed while I lived in
the State.   In 1824, I think it was, LaFayette was looked for in Alabama.   I was the first and oldest Brigadier
General in Alabama, (after it became a State.) Gen.
Wm. Taylor, I think, was the oldest Major General; and
Israel Pickens was Governor.   There may have been his
equal, but there never has been his superior in that office
since Alabama became a State.   At the time LaFayette
was expected, Gen. Taylor was absent, I think, in Mobile.
The Indians were a little soured, from a treaty that had
been, or was about being made with the Georgians.   Gov.
Pickens requested me to take an escort and conduct
LaFayette through the nation.   The Hon. James Aber-
crombie then commanded the Montgomery Troop, and
Gen. Moore of Claiborne, commanded the Monroe Troop,
both of whom volunteered their services.   Before the
escort left Alabama, (which then extended only to Line
Creek,) Gen. Taylor arrived and took the command.

That was before the day of platforms and conventions—
men lived on their own money. You must guess then
there was some patriotic feeling along, for there were between two and three hundred persons, all bearing their

own expences. Some in going and coming had to travel
four hundred milas, and none less than two hundred miles.
Besides the military, there were a number of the most
respectable citizens of Alabama—among whom were
Boling Hall, ex-member of Congress, ex-Gov. Murphy,
John D. Bibb, John W. Freeman and Col. James John-
ston, one of the best men that ever lived or died. If
there are any such men these days, I have not had the
pleasure of their acquaintance. Our trip to the Chattahoochee was pleasant indeed. We made our head-quarters three miles from Fort Mitchell, on big Uchee Creek,
at Haynes Crabtree's. Had that been a war, and if it had
continued till the present day, all of that crowd that's
now living would be soldiers. After some three or four
days' stay at Crabtree's, we learned that Gen. LaFayette
had passed White Water, and we knew at what time he
would reach the river. The Indians seemed to take as
much interest in the matter as the whites. All hands
mustered on the west or Alabama side, where we could
see the Georgia escort approach the east bank of the
Chattahoochee, with their charge. On the east bank,
Gen. LaFayette was met by Chilly McIntosh, son of the
Indian Gen. McIntosh, with fifty Indian warriors, who
were stripped naked and finely painted. They had a
sulky prepared with drag-ropes, such as are commonly
used in drawing cannon. The General was turned over
by the Georgians to the Indians. That was the greatest
show I ever saw at the crossing of any river. It beat all
of Gen. Jessup's wind bridges across the Tallapoosa, and
other places where there was never much more water
than would swim a dog, only at a high rise. As the ferry-
boat reached the Alabama side, the Indians, in two lines,
seized the ropes, and the General seated in the sulky,
was drawn to the top of the bank, some eighty yards,
where stood the Alabama Delegation. At a proper distance from the Alabama Delegation, the Indians opened
their lines, and the sulky halted.

Everything, from the time the General entered the

ferry, till this time, had been conducted in the most profound silence. As the sulky halted, the Indians gave
three loud whoops. The General then alighted, took off
his hat, and was conducted by Chilly McIntosh, a few
steps, to where stood Mr. Hall, with head uncovered,
white with the frosts of age. I knew Mr. Hall from my
boyhood. He always showed well in company; but never
did I see him look so finely as on that occasion—he looked like himself—what he really was—an American gentleman. As McIntosh approached Mr. Hall, he said,
"Gen. LaFayette, the American friend"—"Mr. Hall, of
Alabama," pointing to each as he called his name. Mr.
Hall, in a very impressive manner, welcomed LaFayette
to the shores of Alabama, and introduced him to the
other gentlemen. Dandridge Bibb then addressed the
General at some length. I heard a number of persons
address LaFayette on his route through Alabama—none
surpassed Dandridge Bibb, and none equalled him, unless it was Hitchcock and Dr. Hustis at Cahaba. I have
always been looked upon as rather dry-faced; but gazing
on the face of the most distinguished patriot that it had
ever fallen to my lot to look upon, and the feeling remarks of Mr. Bibb on that occasion, caused me, as it did
most others that were present, to shed tears like so many
childen.

After the address at the river, all marched to Fort
Mitchell hill, where there was an immense crowd of Indians, the Little Prince at their head. He addressed the
"French Captain," through Hamley, in true Indian style.
I could understand much of his speech, but cannot begin
to give it as Hamley could. The Prince said that he
had often heard of the French Captain, "but now I see
him, I take him by the hand, I know from what I see, he
is the true one I have heard spoken of; I am not deceived
—too many men have come a long way to meet him. He
is bound to be the very man the Americans were looking for." The Prince, after satisfying the General that
he (the Prince) was satisfied that the General was the

true man spoken of and looked for, then went on to say,
that he had once warred against the Americans, and that
the French Captain had warred for them, and of course
they had once been enemies, but were now friends; that
he (the Prince) was getting old, which his withered limbs
would show—making bare his arms at the same time—
that he could not live long; but he was glad to say, that
his people and the whites were at peace and he hoped
they would continue so.

But he had raised a set of young warriors, that he
thought would prove worthy of their sires, if there should
ever be a call to show themselves men; and that as a ball
play was, outside of war, the most manly exercise that
the Red Man could perform, he would, for the gratification of the General and his friends, make his young men
play a game. The old man then turned to his people,
and said to them—they were in the presence of a great
man and warrior; he had commanded armies on both
sides of the Big Water; that he had seen many nations
of people; that he had visited the Six Nations, in Red
Jacket's time, (the General told the Indians he had visited the Six Nations,) that every man must do his best—
show himself a man, and should one get hurt he must re-
tire without complaining, and by no means show anything
like ill humor. The speech ended, about two hundred
stripped to the buff, paired themselves off and went at it.
It was a ball play sure enough, and I would travel farther
to see such a show than I would to see any other performed by man, and willingly pay high for it, at that.
The play ended, and all hands went out to head quarters
at Big Uchee, where we were kindly treated by our old
friend Haynes Crabtree.

There was a man, then living among the Indians, Capt.
Tom Anthony, who long since found a last resting place
in the wilds of Arkansas. He was a man of fine sense
and great humor. There was also an Indian known as
Whiskey John. John was the greatest drunkard I ever
saw; he would drink a quart of strong whiskey without

5

taking the vessel that contained it from his lips, (this is Alabama history, and there are plenty now living that have seen him do it.) To see John drink was enough to have made the fabled Bacchus look out for a vacancy that frequently occurs among the Sons of Temperance. Capt. Anthony told John that all hands had addressed the French Chief, and that it was his duty to say something to him on behalf of those that loved whiskey. John could speak considerable English in a broken manner. It so happened that the General and others were walking across the Uchee Bridge when John met them. John made a low bow, as he had seen others do. The General immediately pulled off his hat, thinking he had met with another Chief. John straightening himself up to his full height, (and he was not very low,) commenced his speech in the manner that I will try to give it to you. "My friend, you French Chief! me Whiskey John," (calling over the names of several white persons and Indians;) "Col. Hawkins, Col. Crowell, Tom Crowell, Henry Crowell, Billy McIntosh, Big Warrior Indian, heap my friends, give me whiskey, drink, am good. White man my very good friend me, white man make whiskey, drink him heap, very good, I drink whiskey. You French Chief Tom Anthony say me big Whiskey Chief. You me give one bottle full. I drink him good." The General informed John that he did not drink whiskey, but would have his bottle filled. John remarked "Tom Anthony you very good man, me you give bottle full. You no drink, me drink him all, chaw tobacco little bit, give me some you." Now the above is an Indian speech, and no doubt will appear silly to some who have not been accustomed to those people. Should it, however, fall under the eye of those who were along at the time, they will recognize John's speech, and call to mind our old friends, Capt. Anthony and Col. James Johnson, who was the life of our crowd.

We remained that night at Crabtree's and the next day reached Fort Bainbridge, where an Indian country-

man lived, by the name of Kendall Lewis, as perfect a
gentleman, in principle, as ever lived in or out of the
nation, and had plenty, and it in fine style. The next
day we started for Line Creek.

It fell to my lot to point out many Indians, as well as
places, for we were stopped at almost every settlement to
shake hands, and hear Indian speeches. Among many
things and places that were pointed out to the General,
was the place where Lot was killed, the old "Lettered
Beech," at Persimmon swamp, the old Council Oak,
Floyd's battle ground, the grave of James McGirth, the
place where McGirth made peach brandy, many years
before, and many other things. That night we reached
Walter B. Lucas'. Every thing was "done up" better
than it will ever be again; one thing only was lacking
—time—we could not stay long enough. The next
morning we started for Montgomery. Such a cavalcade
never traveled that road before or since.

On Goat Hill,* and near where Capt. John Carr fell in
the well, stood Gov. Pickens, and the largest crowd I
ever saw in Montgomery. Some hundred yards east of
the Hill, was sand flat, where Gen. LaFayette and his
attendants quit carriages and horses, formed a line and
marched to the top of the hill. As we started, the band
struck up the old Scottish air, "Hail to the Chief." As
we approached the Governor, Mr. Hill introduced the
General to him. The Governor tried to welcome him,
but, like the best man the books give account of, when it
was announced that he was commander of the whole
American forces, he was scarcely able to utter a word.
So it was with Gov. Pickens. As I remarked before,
Gov. P. had no superior in the State, but on that occasion
he could not even make a speech. But that did not prevent Gen. LaFayette from discovering that he was a great
man; it only goes to prove what is often said, that many
who feel most can say least, and many who have no feeling say too much.

* The site of the present Capitol of Alabama.　　　　H.

The people of Montgomery did their duty. Col. Arthur Hayne, who was a distinguished officer in the army in the war of 1813, and who was the politest gentleman I ever saw, was the principal manager. If the Earl of Chesterfield had happened there he would have felt as I did the first time I saw a fine carpet on a floor and was asked to walk in; I declined, saying, "I reckon I have got in the wrong place." Several steamboats were in waiting at the wharf, and the next morning all hands went aboard and started for Cahaba, at that time the Seat of Government.

At Cahaba, as in Montgomery, everything was "done up" as it should be. There the General met with Major Porter, whom he had known in the Revolution. There I shed more tears. The General examined the old ditch that had been cut by his countrymen many years before. An old cannon was shown him also, which was left by the French Army, when they quit the country. He remarked that those relics caused sad feelings, that there was still a pleasure, a kind of melancholy pleasure, which he could not describe.

About this time a gentleman was wounded from the firing a cannon on a trading boat. The General visited the wounded man, and took much interest in his welfare; he was told that the gentleman had many friends who would care for him; I told him that he was an old camp mate of mine; he replied, "one good soldier will always take care of another." I remained in Cahaba until the General embarked on board a steamboat for Mobile; I accompanied him on board, and on bidding him farewell, said, "I have done what little I could to make your journey to this place as pleasant as possible, and I now have to leave you." He took me by the hand and said, "I thank you kindly; may God bless and prosper the young and thriving State you live in; I shall always cherish the kindest feelings for you and the other gentlemen that escorted me through the nation, as well as all others who have taken so much trouble to make me welcome among

you." The last words I heard him utter were, "Farewell,
my friend! Take care of that wounded man."

Yours,

T. S. W.

WHEELING, WINN PARISH, LA., ⎱
August 12th, 1858. ⎰

COL. ALBERT J. PICKETT.

Dear Sir:—In my letter to you of the 21st June last,
which was published in the Montgomery Mail of the
23d July, I see a mistake that I will here correct. In
speaking of Davy Tate, it is said he was not an educated man. Mr. Tate *was* an educated man; and, if I
am not mistaken, he informed me that he was educated near Abernethy, in Scotland, and was about ten
years younger than Alexander McGillivray. As I may
at some time after this, speak more of Mr. Tate and
his half brother, Weatherford, I will leave them here,
and give you some of my reasons for having said to
Mr. Hooper, in a letter some time back, that I was
more inclined to credit the Indian tradition of DeSoto's
expedition through the country, than those Spanish
and Portuguese authors.

Before I commence with the Indian account of De-
Soto's travels through Georgia, Alabama, Mississippi,
Arkansas, and Louisiana, I will point out a few things,
among the many, that those Spanish and Portuguese
gentry have grossly erred in. They may appear to you
and others as very trivial objections. But they are errors; and if a man willfully misrepresents one thing,
he will another; and if he does it ignorantly once, he
is liable to do it again. And as I alluded to the killing of
a panther, the raising of hogs on the road, the building of
brigantines, I will here speak more of these things.

The history says that the Spanish captive, Jean Ortez,
one night, while guarding the Indian tombs or the dead

Indians, killed a panther trying to carry off a dead child. This story does not only prove that they wrote falsely, but that they were poor zoologists; for the panther is an animal that never preys upon putrid flesh. This is a fact known to every hunter, from the days of the grand-son of Ham, down to the Englishman, Boone, the early hunter of Kentucky; Mike Shuck, of Missouri; Albert Pike and Kit Carson, of the plains of New Mexico; Winthrop Colbreath, of the Caddo Mountains of Arkansas: to John L. Winston, of Texas. Besides, the Indians that I have been acquainted with, all inhabited countries that were infested with wolves and other animals which prey upon their dead, if left exposed, and always guarded against such. And putting their dead in boxes, leaving them above the earth, is a thing I never heard of before. All that is necessary to refute the hog story, for sensible men—who know anything of hog-raising, the time they go with their young, the time it requires for them to be fit for use, and this to be done on a farm where every necessary preparation is made for raising them—is to read the narrative, notice the country they traveled through, the many rivers they had to cross—and the Mississippi among them—then the quantity of those animals left behind for the successor of DeSoto, and his men to kill and pack away, (and if packed at all, must have been without salt;) all I ask is, to examine the account given by those men, and then say if there is the slightest probability of its being true. Now, the building of seven brigantines, in the short space of seven months, fitting them out, rigging them up with sails made of Indian mantles, with the means they had for carrying on such work—this, if not a palpable fiction, is a very improbable story, particularly when we take into consideration that these vessels were made sea-worthy, and had to descend the Mississippi river from some point in Arkansas to the Gulf, and then across to some point on the coast of Mexico. It is a tale that will do to tell to marines, but old sailors, old seamen and ship carpenters, will never believe it to be true. The stories of the fine specimens of pearls and martin skins being found in the country, are equally fabulous with the others. Pearls are not to be found at the present day, nor ever have been since I knew or heard of the country; and the martin is an animal that never inhabited the country. And there is very little probability of there being any trade at that day so advantageous, among the Southern Indians, as would induce the Northern Indians (in whose country a few martins might have been found) to trade at such a great distance from home, on martin skins alone—for almost all the other animals that Indians hunted for their flesh and skins, were in as great, if not greater, abundance in the south and south-west, than in any other portion of what is now the United States. If you will notice in many of the minor occurrences of the expedition, they give the day and date, month and year; but no date is given when the hero of the expedition dies. Now if those that have made mention of DeSoto's dying at some point in Arkansas had known the time he did die, they would in all probability have given us the precise time, as well as the place of his decease. From the Indian tradition and from what those men wrote who returned to Europe, I think it more than probable they never knew what became of DeSoto and the few men that were with him when he did die. Fable is fable, and history is history and those men thought it best to mix them as they were writing for a people not unlike many of the present day—who never look into books unless it is for pictures and the marvelous yarns it contains. I will now give you the Indian account of the expedition.

DeSoto commenced his march from Tampa Bay; and the first winter camped on the Apalachicola river, near Ocheese. Which place has been known in my time as Spanny-Wakee—that is the Spanish camp, or the Spaniards lay there. Their object was gold. They there divided their force into several commands under various individuals, marching in a northerly direction, through portions of Georgia and Alabama. The Indians say that none of

DeSoto's men ever crossed to the east of the Oconee river, unless it was some of its head branches. A portion of the Spaniards made their way up the Chattahoochee to Owe-Cowka, or the shoals of Columbus; there they called a halt, until they could correspond with the others that had gone farther east and north. Tallapoosa was then known as the river of towns; Tuckabatchee being the most important town in the nation, except Cusseta, was the point for the different commands to meet at. A portion of them had traveled the route through northern Georgia, as you describe, and then a south-westerly course, through a portion of Alabama, reaching the Tallassees who then occupied a portion of what is now Talladega. Their principal town was on a creek that bears their name to this day, by the Indians. In this time, the Spaniards had become obnoxious to the Indians; particularly those that had been quartered about where Columbus now is. This party left the Chattahoochee for Tuckabatchee and traveled pretty much the route that now leads from Columbus to Pole Cat Springs; their trail or trace passed through Tuskegee, and has been known as DeSoto's trace ever since. I knew the country long before, and many that are now living knew it, as DeSoto's trace. The party that took this route missed their way, and instead of going to Tuckabatchee they reached the Tallapoosa lower down, where the Indians disputed their passage, and a fight ensued. The place they fought at took its name from the fight, Thlea Walla or Rolling Bullet; it is sometimes called Cuwally, and at others Hothleawally, by many, but Thlea Walla is the proper name. And it was at this place, no doubt, that that greatly exaggerated Maubile fight took place; and I will give you many good reasons for believing it. In the first place, the Indians never gave an account of any other fight with Tustanugga Hatke or White Warrior, as they called DeSoto. Another reason is that the Tallassees or Tallaces, at that time evidently occupied a portion of Talladega; and from Talladega down to Thleawalla about suits the distance that they would have had to travel. It was in Talladega that the Tallasses lived; and it must have been at that point where the invitation from Tuscaloosa was received by DeSoto. I have remarked somewhere long before this that the Tuckabatchy town, on Tallapoosa, was settled at least two centuries before the Tallasees settled the town that they left in 1836. I now say to you, without the fear of being contradicted by any one that knows, that the Tallasses never settled on the Tallapoosa river before 1756; they were moved to that place by James McQueen— McQueen settling himself at the same time near where Walter Lucas once had a stand, at the crossing of Line Creek; and it was at that place on Line Creek where the celebrated negro interpreter, John McQueen, was born. The Tallasses quit their old settlements in the Talladega country, and it was immediately occupied by a band of Netches, under the control of a chief called Chenubby, and a Hollander by the name of Moniac. This man was the father of Sam Moniac, whom you in your History call McNae, thinking him to be of Scotch race. The chief Chennubby lived to be a very old man. I knew him as well as I did any Indian in the Nation. He was with Gen. Jackson in the Creek War; he was with me in Florida in 1818. I have often by a camp fire sat and listened to him tell over his troubles among the French, on the Mississippi, and how the French had drove them from their old homes; and how he had helped to drive the French from their trading house at the forks of Coosa and Tallapoosa. It was his son, young Chennubby or Sarlotta Fixico, who left Fort Leslie and went to Gen. Jackson's camp. The story of the hog-skin over the Indian, is all a hoax.

But to return to the Spaniards. You see they speak of Coosa and Tallase; those names are easy to pronounce; and they no doubt visited those towns; but you never hear Tuckabatchy named, for they were not at the place. It was at Thlea Walla that the Indians picked up those copper and brass plates that you have heard spoken of. The

Indians say that after DeSoto failed to find gold in
the mountain countries of Georgia and Alabama, he
steered his course a little north of west for the Mississippi;
that his people divided; some turned to the seaboard and
were picked up by the coasting vessels; some starved, and
many died with disease; that DeSoto himself, with a small
portion of his men, some Creeks, some Mauhile or Movilla
Indians, some Choctaws and others, tried to reach Mexico. He promised the Indians that accompanied him that
he could make a peace with them and Cortez, or those
Spaniards that had driven them from their old homes.
And not far from a small lake and west of Red River, he
built a fort to protect himself from the Netches, Natchitoches and Nacogdaches Indians; that he there died.
This is the account given by all the Indians, and those
that were acquainted with their traditions relative to the
march of DeSoto through the country. The fort is yet
very visible, and is known as the Azadyze; it is in Natchitoches Parish, in this State. This was Col. Silas Dins-
more's account, obtained from the Choctaws and Chica-
saws, who was their agent at an early day, and a man of
great intelligence. It was also the account that old Mr.
Peechland gave, who lived among them many years. The
Creek Indians say they once had a giant chief called Tustanugga Lusta or Black Warrior. But Tusca Loosa is a
mixed word of Creek and Choctaw. Tusca is Creek, and
signifies a warrior—Loosa is Choctaw, and signifies black.
But whether it was this man that fought DeSoto, I never
heard; but have always understood that at Thlea Walla
was the place they fought. The old French and Spanish
settlers on Red River said that the descendants of DeSoto's
men were among the natives when those nations (that is
France and Spain) first commenced settling Louisiana.
All this has satisfied me that Indians were more reliable
in their traditions of that expedition than men that have
written so much, and in so few instances have given the
true Indian character as well as their modes of living.
And why I am better satisfied that the Maubile fight took

its origin from the Thlea Walla fight, is that there were but few remains of Indian settlements on the Alabama river below the mouth of Cahawba, and they were very small. The Coosa, Tallapoosa, and Chattahoochee and their waters were very thickly settled with Indians at an early day. The Maubile or Movillas were once a western people, but visited and settled Alabama before the Creeks did. There is yet a language the Texas Indians call the Mobilian tongue, that has been the trading language of almost all the tribes that have inhabited the country. I know white men that now speak it. There is a man now living near me that is fifty years of age, raised in Texas, that speaks the language well. It is a mixture of Creek, Choctaw, Chickasay, Netches and Apelash.

From the time Columbus discovered the country, until DeSoto's expedition, was near a half century; and almost all the European nations that had shipping had become acquainted with the New World, and no doubt but the most of DeSoto's men that survived and reached the coast were picked up by coasting vessels, as the Indians have said. This is much more probable than that they (the Spaniards) built brigantines for that purpose. And no doubt there were occasional settlements on the coast at that time by Europeans—for Dr. Turnbull on settling a colony of Minorcans or Greeks in East Florida, south-west of St. Augustine, found the remains of civilization that the oldest natives then could give no account of. Turnbull made this settlement while the English claimed Florida. And when Lasalle settled a small colony in Texas, many years before Turnbull settled his, he (Lasalle) found the remains of civilization that he never could learn from the natives at what time or by whom they were executed. I read these accounts in a little book I picked up at the house of one Fashaw. in East Florida, forty-six years back. I kept the book for many years; it contained much useful information, and treated much of the early settlements in the South-West by Europeans—and much of what it contained I have heard corroborated by others.

Yours,
T. S. W.

———

WHEELING, WINN PARISH, LA.,
September 16th, 1858.

To J. J. HOOPER, ESQ:

Dear Sir—I do not take my pen in hand according to the old custom, but have it between my thumb and fore-finger, and you can judge whether or not it improves my hieroglyphics. And as I have at times been detailing to you some few things about Indians and Indian customs, one thing I learned from them—that time was never an object with them; and at this time must follow their example—take my time.

* * * * * * * * * *

I received a letter the other day from my worthy friend, the Knight of the Horse-Shoe. I speak nothing but the truth when I say that I am truly glad to hear that he is still living and in good health. I hope he may live as long as suits his convenience. I don't know that I would care if he could live a thousand years, and die rich, so that I could be left to administer his estate. But he and myself will settle up long before that time, and put out; and if I continue in these piney-woods and it does not rain more, so that I can make better crops than I am making this year, I may make it convenient to die my own executor; or, at least, leave a very little job on hand for those that would undertake the settlement of my affairs.

My friend writes me that your city is improving, and that he is the only one left that settled at Montgomery as early as himself—that, I think, was in 1817. Arthur Moore, the first white man that built a house and lived in it at Motgomery, built it in the latter part of 1815, or early in 1816. The cabin stood upon the bluff above what was once called the ravine, and not far from where Gen. Scott put up a steam mill. The spot where the cabin stood had gone into the river before I left the country. And a man by the name of Tom Moore was the first settler at Selma. These are things that I know, and no matter who knows to the contrary. This is not very interesting, but as the names of the first settlers of many places have been handed down, from the first settling of the fruit garden to the present time, it will do no injury to either Montgomery or Selma to know their first settlers.

I am glad to learn that your city, as well as the State, is improving. Alabama is very little in advance of what she should have been, when we look back and see who were its early settlers. No State that has come into the Union since the old thirteen, at its early settlement, equalled Alabama as to intellect or large planting interests. Alabama ought to lay off a county at least, in some important part of the State, and call it Abner McGehee; and the people of Montgomery particularly should make some mark to show to that posterity so often spoken of, that such a man as Abner McGehee had lived. I hope Alabama will continue to follow the example of her older sister—my native State—Georgia. All hands say they trust in kind Providence; and should it deny me the pleasure of ever visiting Alabama, I shall while I live cherish the kindest feelings for her, and particularly Montgomery and Selma, and more particularly that Queen of country villages, Tuskegee.

I have received the Columbus paper that my friend Ned sent me. I notice the letter of a person that I recollect to have seen over forty years ago, and think I contributed a little in relieving that person from one of the most pitiable situations that it ever falls to the lot of a human being to be placed in. And I am sorry that one who in early life witnessed so many horrors, should in old age be reduced to destitution*. Say to my friend that I hope I

---

* This refers to Mrs. Dill, to whom Gen. Woodward sent a sum of money. He was one of those who rescued her from the Indians, in 1818.   H.

know my duty, and had I not learned in early life to sympathise with and for the widow and orphan, that his many kind examples would long since have taught me my duty.

I not long since received a letter purporting to be written by one George D. Taylor. I know it is not Col. George Taylor, of Coosa, for he is my friend and a gentleman. If there be such a man as George D. Taylor, and he writes to me again, I will beg permission to answer him through your paper, and will pledge myself to give as true a history of a person that he claims to be related to, as any one can give him that now lives. * * *

Yours truly,
T. S. W

——

WHEELING, WINN PARISH, LA.,
Oct. 20th, 1858.

To J. J. HOOPER, ESQ.

Dear Sir :—Whenever a biographer, or one who writes sketches of the lives of others, no matter whether they be true or false, so long as he speaks in praise of the individual of whom he writes, he never can be charged with maliciously doing wrong, unless, by chance or otherwise, he raises the reputation of his hero at the expense of another. But if an individual from the best of motives, undertakes to correct errors to set mankind right in relation to the true history of men and things, he is often charged with being influenced by, or from, malicious motives, or something worse; particularly should he write any thing that would be the least calculated to dim in a small degree the lustre thrown around some favorite by a good hearted, visionary biographer. But no truly conscientious man while living, could brook the idea of thanking a man, that after he was dead, would emblazon to the world a fame he was not entitled to, or ascribe to him deeds of daring that he had not performed while living. For what I am now going to write, I will no doubt be censured by some. But what need I care, for I am now old, and it will not be long before I appear at a place where a life time of truth will be worth more to me than all the good or bad opinions entertained of me by those I leave behind. I have just been looking over Col. Pickett's sketches relative to Gen. Sam Dale. And I find them so utterly incorrect, and the history of the man (by Col. P.) so entirely different from what I know it to have been, or know it to be, I must at least be allowed to say, that the Colonel has a very fruitful imagination, or has been most egregiously imposed upon, or perhaps both. But in justice to Col. Pickett, I must say, if I knew a man with little merit, that had seen one hostile Indian, a few teeth pulled out, a few eyes and noses operated on, and a few fingers amputated, who wished his life written while living or after he was dead, and it praised according to the most approved style, by modern light readers, I would reccommend him to the Colonel, or the Colonel to him. For taking into consideration the subject of the Colonel's memoirs and the material he has had left him to work with, he can certainly color a picture as high as it will bear at least. I knew Gen. Dale before Col. P. was born, and knew him through life, and knew him well : none knew him better, and to give a true sketch of his life, would be to go back to Georgia and detail a hundred or more fist fights, and down to his last fight in Georgia, which was with John Wesley Webb, in Clinton, Jones county. Those who knew Gen. Dale, will recollect the scars on his face; they were the flesh marks of John Wesley Webb. Dale was an Indian trader, and traded with the Upper Towns in the Creek Nation, some of which I will name : the Ocfuskes, Cieligces, Fish Ponds or Tatloulgees, Hillabys, Netches, Talladegas, or the people of the border. His principal partner was Col. Harrison Young. The half-breed that Col. Pickett alludes to as his partner, was his interpreter, by the name of John Berfort or Berford, and partly raised by Gen. Adams. If Dale was ever a Colonel in the Georgia line and killed two Indians at Ocfuske, on the Chattahoochee, I never heard of it. There was a trading path that crossed Chattahoochee going to Ocfuske on the Tallapoosa, and a few Indians traded at it; but the only Ocfuske town in my time was at Tallapoosa. The Horse Shoe was called Ocfuske. In point, I recollect Col. Fosh, he was once the Adjutant General of Georgia; the Georgians called him a Frenchman, but he was a Polander, and unfortunately for him and his men, the records giving an account of his exploits in Indian fighting have been lost. The only, or principal fight with whites and Creek Indians, between the Revolution and the War of 1813–14, that has been left on record, was Clark's fight at Jack's Creek; though there were some killed on both sides, before and after that. Not long after the fight with Webb, which I think was in 1810, Dale and Young moved to Mississippi Territory, near St. Stephens. It is a mistake about Dale being at the Indian Council at Tuckabatchy in 1811, at the time of Tecumseh's visit; and it is also a mistake about his having communicated to Col. Hawkins what was considered to be the object of Tecumseh's visit among the Crecks. For the Colonel had spies in the nation that watched the movements of him and the Big Warrior, and Billy McIntosh was one of them, and no white man was admitted into their councils; and could it now be ascertained to a certainty, I would hazard anything I have that Tecumseh, Seekaboo and their few followers were never seen by a half dozen white men that knew them, from the time they left the Wabash until they returned to the Warpicanatta Village. Christian Limbo, John Ward, Bob Walton and Nimrod Doyle saw Tecumseh at the Tallassee Square, opposite Tuckabatchy, and the reason why they were permitted to see him, was, that Walton and Doyle had known him in his younger days. These men have described Tecumseh to me minutely, and what well satisfies me they did so, I lived neighbor to the late Col. Clever of Arkansas, who was a Lieutenant in the last war, or war of 1812, and was at the battle of the

Thames. It will be recollected by those who knew Col. Clever that he was a great friend of Col. Johnson, but denied him the credit of killing Tecumseh. He said Tecumseh was killed some time after Col. Johnson was wounded and disabled; that he was killed at least three hundred yards from where the Colonel was shot. And while I am at it, I will go into a minute detail of Col. Clever's statement, as it corroborates the statement made by Doyle and Walton. He said, from the way the Indians rallied and fought around a certain Indian until he was killed, and a small trinket found on his person, that he was supposed to be a Chief. And there being but few if any among the whites that had known Tecumseh, except Gen. Harrison, it was some time after the close of the fight before it was ascertained that the dead Chief was Tecumseh; and it was only ascertained through the General. The circumstance of the bold stand made by the supposed Chief being communicated to Gen. Harrison, he visited the spot where the dead Indian lay; the body was much mangled, and as the General approached the spot a soldier was in the act of taking off a piece of skin from the Indian's thigh. The General ordered the soldier to stop, and said he regretted to know that he had such a man in his camp, and reprimanded him severely. He had some water brought, had the Indian washed and stretched his full length, examined his teeth and pronounced it to be Tecumseh. One of Tecumseh's legs was a little shorter than the other, and the foot on the short leg a little smaller, and he had a halt in his walk that was perceptible, and he had a tooth, though not decayed, of a bluish cast. This was Col. Clever's statement, that I have heard him make a hundred times; and his description corroborates that of Doyle and Walton, of Tecumseh. At all events, Tecumseh was killed at the battle of the Thames; history, or some portion of it, gives the credit to Col. Johnson; I have given Col. Clever's account of that affair, without giving my opinion as to who killed him. And there is but one man that I know

6

of living that could give any satisfactory evidence of that matter—it is Gen. Lewis Cass, the present Secretary of State, of the United States.

I will now go back to where I am better acquainted. Gen. Dale was in the Burnt Corn battle, but from what I have learned from the late Judge Lipscomb, of Texas, formerly of Alabama, and others, on the part of the whites, and Jim Boy, the principal War Chief, that was with McQueen, and whom Col. P. styles "High Head Jim," the whole affair was but a light one. The Canoe Fight was reality—I knew all the party, that is, Gen. Dale, Col. Austill, James Smith and the negro Caesar. Col. Austill is yet living, and of course knows more of the fight than I can possibly know. But I have no doubt that he will say that the fight has been detailed by Col. Pickett to the best advantage for those engaged in it; and will also say that an Indian fight, either in a canoe or the bushes, alters its appearance very much by getting into a book or newspaper. I have heard the accounts given, from Gen. Dale down to Ceasar; it's a pity the eight big Indians killed in the canoe had not been taken to the shore for the landsmen to have looked at. Col. Pickett says a few years before that, that Gen. Dale was in the act of drinking, when two Indians tried to tomahawk him; that he knifed them, took their trail carrying five bleeding wounds, brained three more warriors, released a female prisoner and she killed the fourth. That's another exploit I never heard of. I suspect the woman's dead by now; and whether this startling event was in the Georgia wars between the Revolution and the war of 1813–14, or at what period or place, we are not told. The account only says some years before the Canoe fight. I could not help smiling when I read the Colonel's account of the Roman Consul, Acquilius, and comparing a case of Gen. Dale's in Mobile to that of the Consul's. Silence, I think, would have been the strongest appeal that persons in their situations could have made, particularly in Mobile, and would have evinced more greatness in both the Gen-

eral and Consul. Now, sir, let me tell you who General
Dale was and what he was: he was honest, he was brave,
he was kind to a fault, his mind was of the ordinary kind,
not well cultivated, fond of speculation and not well fit-
ted for it ; a bad manager in money matters and often
ebarrassed, complained much of others for his misfortunes;
was very combative, always ready to go into danger;
would hazard much for a friend and was cha ritable in
pecuniary matters. even to those he looked upon as enemies. I could relate many little frolics of his that might
be interesting to a few, but as such things are witnessed
almost daily, particularly where whiskey is drunk, I shall
not mention them. He spent much of his time with me
in 1834. He knew very little about Indian character, and
entertained a good feeling for that persecuted people. So
soon as he had an enemy in his power he was done, and
would sympathise with and for him, and at times would cry
like a child. I have given you the true character of Gen.
Dale, and those that were old enough and were intimately
acquainted with him, will tell you I have given a faithful
account of the man as far as I have gone. What I have written is to correct error, not to detract, and you never can
take from a man that which he never had. What Col.
Pickett has written of Gen. Dale and others that I know,
would do for a novel, but not history. Men who write
history and wish to deal a little in the marvelous for the
amusement of readers, should look around and see who
is living, particularly if they are writing about things tnat
have happened in their own time, and a little before.

I will, in a day or two, write out and send you the
true character of Billy Weatherford and the part he acted
in the war—some things I personally know, and others
I obtained from Weatherford himself, and he was truly
what the Indians called him. Billy Larney, or Yellow
Billy, was one of his names; his other was Hoponica-
futsahia, or Truth Maker or Teller. And as Col. Pickett
has failed to give us a history of the war of 1836-7, in
Alabama, and as I participated with him and others in

that memorable struggle to see who could get first into Mr. Belser's paper, and for fear some may die off and not do it, I will write that out and send it to you.

It will be seen that I have alluded to Col. Johnson, and that there are doubts as to his killing Tecumseh; it matters not who killed Tecumseh, Col. Johnson proved himself a distinguished man, not only as a soldier, but in everything else that he has undertaken. And that is a subject I should not have alluded to here, but I see in Col. Pickett's history that he says Gen. Dale saw Tecumseh at the Council with the Creek Indians in 1811, which I am certain is incorrect. Persons that have not read Col. Picket's history of Alabama, will lose much of my meaning. And notwithstanding many of the Colonel's pictures are highly wrought and his information and knowledge of the modern Creeks and their war with the whites in 1813–14, are very imperfect, his history is very well written, and will be found by those who have not read it an interesting work. I will close this by simply remarking that it matters not whose reputation history raises, or whose character it damages, it is the duty of all that can do so, to correct its errors.

Respectfully,
T. S. W.

———

WHEELING, WINN PARISH, LA.,
October 31st, 1858.

TO J. J. HOOPER, ESQ:

Dear Sir: Some months back I addressed a letter to Mr. Rutherford of Union Springs, containing some of the incidents of the life of Billy Weatherford. Not having seen it published, I have concluded to give you a few sketches of the history of that man and the part he took in the war of 1813–14. His father was Charles Weatherford, a white man, that came to the Creek Nation shortly after the close of the American Revolution, in company with Sam Mimms, who was once engaged with George

Galphin in the Indian trade. Weatherford's mother was
a half breed Tuskegee, her father was a Scotchman by the
name of Malcolm McPherson, and a blood relation to the
late Judge Berrien, of Georgia. Seboy or Sehoya Mc-
Pherson was brought up in her early days by the father
of Sam Moniac. She lived a part of her time with Lauchlan McGillivray and Daniel McDonald. Her first husband was Col. John Tate, the last agent the English had
among the Creeks. By Tate she had one son, Davy, who
is remembered by many who are yet living. Davy Tate
was a man of fine sense, great firmness and very kind to
those with whom he was intimate, and remarkably char-
itable to strangers. But circumstances caused Tate to
mix but little with the world after, the country fell into
the hands of the whites, and he never was well known by
but few after that. I have stated to you before that Col.
Tate died deranged between Flint River and Chattahoochee, and was buried near old Cuseta. Charles Weatherford was the second and last husband of Sehoy Mc-
Pherson. They raised four children that I knew. Betsy,
the oldest child, married Sam Moniac, and was the mother
of Major David Moniac, who was educated at West Point
and was killed by the Seminoles in the fall of 1836—he
was educated at West Point in consequence of the faithful and disinterested friendship of his father to the whites.
Billy was the next oldest, Jack next, and a younger
daughter whose name I have forgotten. She married
Capt. Shumac, a very intelligent officer of the United
State army. I had seen Billy Weatherford before the
war, but only knew him from character. The circumstance of him and Moniac aiding Col. Hawkins in the
arrest of Bowles, made them generally known to the people of Georgia who wished to know anything about Indians. It would be too tedious to tell how I first became
acquainted with Weatherford. I was with Gen. Floyd
in the Nation, and was at his night fight at Calebee; a
few days after the fight the army returned to Fort Hull.
The time was about expiring for which the troops had to

serve, and a call was made for volunteers to take charge of the fort until the Militia from the two Carolinas could arrive. Cap. John H. Broadnax, a very efficient and popular captain, from Putnam county, Georgia, soon raised a company of infantry; a Lieutenant Adaroin from Franklin county raised a rifle corps, and I volunteered as his Orderly Sergeant. A few days before that, the present Gen. Twiggs, then a Captain in the regular army, had forced his way through to the army with his company. The army left, and the three companies above mentioned took charge of the Fort, Col. Homer V. Milton in command. All I recollret to have done myself was to take some authority that one of my rank was not entitled to, under the rules and articles of war, and Capt. Twiggs put me in stocks. And for fear you may think the case worse than it was, I will say to you that I only rendered another Sergeant unfit for duty. I think the whole story would amuse you if you could hear it, but it would be too long for the present; I may give it to you hereafter. I was in the stocks but a few minutes before I was released, and I think after that I was rather a favorite both with the Captain and Colonel. The Colonel wanted an express sent to Gen. Graham at Fort Mitchell. It had to be taken on foot; I volunteered my services, and got George Lovitt, a tall half breed; and obtained a pair of shoes from an Irishman by the name of James Gorman, whom I had known near two years before that in Florida, in the Spanish Patriot service, under my old and intimate friend, Billy Cone. The distance was only forty-five miles. Lovitt and I went in one night, got everything ready and returned to Fort Hull the next night. The troops began to arrive at the Fort, and the Militia under Capt. Broadnax and Lieut. Adaroin, were permitted to leave for home. Col. Milton employed me to go to Fort Hawkins and bring a horse and some baggage left with Col. Cook, which I did. On my return, I found the Colonel at Fort Decatur. On the receipt of his horse and baggage, he gave me a very substantial Indian pony, and proposed to me to remain with him until he reached his regiment, the old 3d Infantry, then at Alabama Heights, under the command of Lieut. Col. Russell, and that he could procure me the appointment of Lieutenant in the army, to be attached to his regiment. I was not ambitious of military honors, and concluded to join the Indians. I had been paid for my services in the previous campaign, had a pony, and that was all I needed. I made up a mess with Sam Sells, John Winslet, Billy McIntosh, Joe Marshall, Sam Moniac and others, and went where it suited me. This gave me an orportunity of becoming acquainted with all the little hostile bands and their leaders. As I have described to you before how the most of them were situated after Gen. Jackson reached the fork of the two rivers, Coosa and Tallapoosa, it will not be necessary now to do so. Though Weatherford was still at Moniac's Island when I reached Gen. Jackson's camp, Tom Carr, or Tuskegee Emarthla, came·up and learned through Moniac that Billy Weatherford could come in with safety, as Col. Hawkins had taken it upon himself to let the General know who and what he, Weatherford, was. I one day went out with Sucky Cornells and others to Cornells' old cow pens to see Jim Boy and Paddy Welch, who had been one of the principal leaders in the fight against Gen. Floyd. Welch was afterwards hanged near Claiborne, for killing a man by the name of Johnson, and another by the name of McCaskill or McCorkell. Jim Boy's camp was not far from Pole Cat Springs, on the Cubahatchy, and near where he built a little town after that which was called Thlopthlocco. On our return to camp, Weatherford, Tom Carr, Otis Harjo, Catsa Harjo or Mad Tiger, a Coowersartda Chief, and a host of others had come in; so I missed hearing the great speech or seeing Ben Baldwin's white horse or the deer. The horse I never heard of, nor him, until I found him in Col. Pickett's history of Alabama. There was a talk with the General and Weatherford and some Chiefs, and of course I did not hear it as I was not permitted to be at head

quarters at that day, being looked upon as another Indian.
But I think I know the purport of the talk as well as any
one living or dead, for I knew both the men well, long after
that, and have heard both of them talk it over; and I
will give you, as near as I can, what I understood passed
at their first interview.   Gen. Jackson said to Weatherford, that he was astonished at a man of his good sense,
and almost a white man, to take sides with an ignorant
set of savages, and being led astray by men who professed
to be prophets and gifted with a supernatural influence.
And more than all, he had led the Indians and was one
of the prime movers of the massacre at Fort Mimms.
Weatherford listened attentively to the General until he
was through.   He then said to the General, that much
had been charged to him that he was innocent of, and that
he believed as little in Indian or white prophets as any
man living, and that he regretted the unfortunate destruction of Fort Mimms and its inmates as much as he, the
General, or any one else.   He said it was true he was at
Fort Mimms when the attack was made, and it was but
a little while after the attack was made before the hostile
Indians seemed inclined to abandon their undertaking;
that those in the Fort, and particularly the half breeds
under Dixon Bailey, poured such a deadly fire into their
ranks as caused them to back out for a short time; at
this stage of the fight he, Weatherford, advised them to
draw off entirely.   He then left to go some few miles to
where his half brother, Davy Tate, had some negroes, to
take charge of them, to keep the Indians from scattering
them; after he left, the Indians succeeded in firing the
Fort, and waited until it burnt so that they could enter
it with but little danger.   He also said to the General
that if he had joined the whites it would have been attributed to cowardice and not thanked.   And moreover,
it was his object in joining the Indians, that he thought
he would in many instances be able to prevent them from
committing depredations upon defenseless persons; and
but for the the mismangement of those that had charge

of the Fort, he would have succeeded, and said, "Now, sir, I have told the truth, if you think I deserve death, do as you please; I shall only beg for the protection of a starving parcel of women and children, and those igno- rant men who have been led into the war by their Chiefs." This is as much as I ever learned from the General, and I will proceed to give Weatherford's own statement, which I have often heard him make. But before I go further, I will here remark why I think the story of the white horse and deer have been played off on the credulity of Col. Pickett, as well as other things I see in his history that I know of my own knowledge, and so do others, to be incorrect. After it was known that Gen. Jackson would punish any one that was known to trouble an In- dian coming to camp unarmed, and particularly Weather- ford, the Indians were put to searching the country for something to eat, particularly those who had been lying out. Moniac was under the impression that he could find some cattle in the neighborhood of his cowpens, on the Pinchong creek. Several Indian countrymen and myself went with the Indians in search of the cattle,— Weatherford went with the crowd, and had to get a horse from Barney Riley, having none of his own; besides, had the exhibition of the white horse and deer been a reality, Major Eaton and others who made speeches for Weather- ford would certainly have noticed it. It has been many years since I read what purported to be Weatherford's speech when he surrendered to Gen. Jackson; but if I recollect right, he was made to say that he would whip the Georgians on one side of the river and make his corn on the other. That was all a lie, and for effect. It re- minds me of the report that the Kentuckians ingloriously fled. It is true, a few Kentuckians had arrived in the neighborhood of New Orleans, when the British made their attack. The Kentuckians were without arms—what could they do? All that can be said is, that it is easier to find a fighting man than a magnanimous one.

I will go back to our cow hunt. At Moniac's cowpens

we found no cattle, but killed plenty of deer and turkeys, and picked up the half brother of Jim Boy—George Goodwin.

Now let us turn to Weatherford. He was a man of fine sense, great courage, and knew much about our government and mankind in general—had lived with his half brother, Davy Tate, who was an educated and well informed man—had been much with his brother-in-law, Sam Moniac, who was always looked upon as being one of the most intelligent half-breeds in the Nation, and was selected by Alexander MiGillivray for interpreter at the time he visited Gen. Washington at New York. Although it has been said that McGillivray mastered the Latin and Greek languages, and although the letters of Alexander Leslie are published to the world as McGillivray's productions, he [McG.] knew too well how matters stood, and relied on Moniac. I have often seen a medal that Gen. Washington gave Moniac. He always kept it on his person, and it is with him in his grave at Pass Christian.

Some time in April, 1814, on the West bank of the Pinchong, now in Montgomery county, Ala., and by a camp fire, I heard Weatherford relate the following particulars about the Creek war:

He said that some few years before the war, a white man came from Pensacola to Tuckabatchy. He remained some time with the Big Warrior. The white man was a European, and he thought a Scotchman; that he never knew the man's business, nor did he ever learn; that all the talks between this man and the Big Warrior were carried on through a negro interpreter that belonged to the Warrior; that he [Weatherford] had seen the man several times, and more than once the man asked how many warriors he thought the Creeks could raise. The man disappeared from the Nation, and in a short time Tuskenea, the oldest son of the Big Warrior, took a trip to the Wabash, and visited several tribes—the Shawnees or Sowanakas. (This trip Tuskenea did make, for I have often heard him speak of it, and have seen some women of the

Hopungiesas and Shawnees that he carried to the Creek Nation.) Weatherford said that not long after the return of Tuskenea to the Creek Nation, Tecumseh, with the Prophet, Seekaboo, and others, made their appearance at the Tuckabatchy town. A talk was put out by the Warrior. Moniac and Weatherford attended the talk. No white man was allowed to be present. Tecumseh stated the object of his mission; that if it could be effected, the Creeks could recover all the country that the whites had taken from them, and that the British would protect them in their right. Moniac was the first to oppose Tecumseh's talk, and said that the talk was a bad one, and that he [Tecumseh] had better leave the Nation. The Big Warrior seemed inclined to take the talk. The correspondence was carried on through Seekaboo, who spoke English. After Moniac had closed, Weatherford then said to Seekaboo to say to Tecumseh, that the whites and Indians were at peace, and had been for years; that the Creek Indians were doing well, and that it would be bad policy for the Creeks, at least, to take sides either with the Americans or English, in the event of a war—(this was in 1811.) Besides, he said, that when the English held sway over the country, they were equally as oppressive as the Americans had been, if not more so; and in the American revolution the Americans were but few, and that they had got the better of the English; and that they were now very strong, and if interest was to be consulted, the Indians had better join the Americans.

After this talk Tecumseh left for home, and prevailed on Seekaboo and one or two others to remain among the Creeks.

In 1812 the Indians killed Arthur Lott and Thomas Meridith, which I before mentioned, as well as Captain Isaacs' going with the Little Warrior to the mouth of Duck river. After this, matters calmed down until the opening of 1813. Moniac and Weatherford took a trip to the Chickasawha in Mississippi Territory, trading in beef cattle. On their return, they found that several chiefs had assembled at a place that was afterwards settled by one Townsend Robinson, from Anson county, N. C. They were taking the Ussa, or black drink, and had Moniac's and Weatherford's families at the square. They told Moniac and Weatherford that they should join or be put to death· Moniac boldly refused, and mounted his horse. Josiah Francis, his brother-in-law, seized his bridle; Moniac snatched a war-club from his hand, gave him a severe blow and put out, with a shower of rifle bullets following him. Weatherford consented to remain. He told them that he disapprobated their course, and that it would be their ruin; but they were his people—he was raised with them, and he would share their fate. He was no chief, but had much influence with the Indians. He was always called by the Indians Billy Larny, or Yellow Billy; that was his boy name. His other name was Hoponika Futsahia. Hoponika Futsahia, as nigh as I can give the English of it, is a truth-maker—and he was all of that.

He then proposed to the Indians to collect up all such as intended going to war with the whites; take their women and children into the swamps ot Florida; leave the old men and lads to hunt for them, and the picked warriors to collect together and operate whenever it was thought best. He said that he had several reasons for making this proposition to the Alabama river Indians: one was, that he thought by the time they could take their women and children to Florida and return, that the upper towns, which were almost to a man hostile,—except the Netches and Hillabys—and were principally controlled by the Ocfuske chief, Menauway, or Ogillis Incha, or Fat Englishman ;— (these were the names of the noted man who headed the Indians at Horse Shoe,)—that they perhaps would come to terms, and by that means his people would be spared and not so badly broken up, and would be the means of saving the lives of many whites on the thinly settled frontiers; and if the worst came to the worst, that they could carry on the war with less trouble, less danger, and less expense, than to be troubled with their women and children.

But in all this he was overruled by the chiefs. Some of their names I will give you. The oldest and principal chief, the one looked upon as the General, was a Tuskegee, called Hopie Tustanugga, or Far-off-Warrior; he was killed at Fort Mims. The others were Peter McQueen, Jim Boy, or High-head Jim, Illes Harjo, or Josiah Francis, the new made Prophet, the Otisee chief, Nehemarthla-Micco, Paddy Welch, Hossa Yohola, and Seekaboo, the Shawnee Prophet, and many others I could name.

The first thing to be had was ammunition. Peter McQueen, with Jim Boy as his war chief, with a party of Indians, started for Pensacola—(their numbers have been greatly overrated.) On their route, at Burnt Corn Springs, they took Betsy Coulter, the wife of Jim Cornells,—(not Alexander Cornells, who was the Government interpreter;) they carried her to Pensacola, and sold her to a French lady, a madame Barrone. At Pensacola they met up with Zach McGirth, and some of them wanted to kill him. Jim Boy interfered, and said that the man or men who harmed McGirth should die.

Now, recollect, I lived with these people long, and have heard these things over and over. Betsy Coulter lived with me for years, as well as others, who bore their parts on one side or the other. This is history—it is as true as Gospel—for I am now and was then a living witness to much of it, and have seen the others who witnessed the balance—and the witnesses to the other have been dead a long time; and besides, what I have seen and write is nothing more than what is and has been common.

But on the return of McQueen's party from Pensacola, the fight took place at Burnt Corn creek between the Indians and at least three times their number of white men; that is, if we take the statements of the two commanders, Col. Collier and Jim Boy. Jim Boy said the war had not fairly broke out, and that they never thought of being attacked; that he did not start with a hundred men, and all of those he did start with were not in the fight.   I have heard Jim tell it often, that if the whites had not stopped to gather up pack horses and plunder their camp, and had pursued the Indians a little further, they [the Indians] would have quit and gone off.   But the Indians discovered the very great disorder the whites were in, searching for plunder, and they fired a few guns from the creek swamp and a general stampede was the result.   McGirth always corroborated Jim Boy's statement as to the number of Indians in the Burnt Corn fight.   I have seen many of those that were in the fight, and they were like the militia that were at Bladensburg—they died off soon; you never could hear much talk about the battle, unless you met with such a man as Judge Lipscomb, who used to make a laughing matter of it.

Enough of the Burnt Corn battle now.   A part of the Indians returned to Pensacola, and some went to the Nation.   So soon as those who had gone back the second time to Pensacola returned, they commenced fitting out an expedition to Fort Mims.   Weatherford said that he delayed them as much as possible on their march, in order that those in the Fort might be prepared.   They took several negroes on the route, and it was made convenient to let them escape; that he had understood that an officer with some troops had reached Fort Mims, and had quite a strong force, but had no expectation of taking it whatever, until the morning they got within view of the Fort; that he was close enough to the Fort to recognize Jim Cornells—saw him as he rode up to the Fort and rode off. I have seen Cornells often since and heard him tell it; he rode to the Fort and told Maj. Beasley that he had seen some Indians, and that the Fort would be attacked that day.   Maj. Beasley was drunk; he said to Cornells that he had only seen a gang of red cattle.   Cornells told the Major that that gang of red cattle would give him a h—ll of a kick before night.   As Cornells rode off, Zach McGirth followed him out, and went to the boat yard; they were looking for a provision boat up, and while McGirth was out the boat was attacked; that is the way he escaped. The Fort gate was open and could not be shut, and a number of the Indians followed a Shawnee (not Seekaboo) who pretended to be a Prophet; he was feathered from top to toe. Dixon Bailey ran up within a few yards of him and placed the Prophet where even the Witch of Endor could not reach him. Some of the Prophet's followers being served in the same way, the rest left the Fort. This I learned from McGirth, Sam Smith and others who were saved and escaped from the Fort, as well as from Jim Boy, Weatherford and others who were engaged in the assault.

The Indians then pretty well ceased operations, and Weatherford, as I have remarked before, left and went off to take charge of his brother's negroes. After he left, the Sawnee, Seekaboo, and some of the McGillivray negroes got behind some logs that were near the Fort, kindled a fire, and, by putting rags on their arrows and setting them on fire, would shoot them into the roof of Mims' smoke-house, which was an old building, and formed a part of one line of the Fort. It took fire and communicated it to the other buildings—and that is the way Fort Mims was destroyed.

Jim Boy succeeded in saving Mrs. McGirth and her daughthr, but her only son, James, was killed. Weatherford's taking charge of Tate's negroes gave rise to the report by some whites that there was an understanding between him and Tate that one was to remain with the whites, and the other with the Indians. The report was, no doubt, false, but it ever after caused Tate to be very reserved with most people. I knew Tate well. He, like Weatherford, was an honest man; but many have done him great injustice.

After the Fort fell, and Jim Boy saved Mrs. McGirth and tried to save others, the Indians ran him off, and it was some time before they would be reconciled to him. After plundering the Fort, they scattered in various directions and made their way back to the Nation, except a few.

The Indians expected after this that the whites would pour into the Nation from all quarters, and most of them that were at Fort Mims returned to where Robinson had a plantation afterwards, and the place that Moniac had escaped from. The reason why they selected that place was, that there was on the North side of the river Nocos-hatchy, or Bear creek, that which afforded the most impenetrable swamps in the whole country. But the movements of the whites were so slow that the Indians grew careless, and a few Indians, with Weatherford and the chief, Hossa Yoholo, and one or two others, made what has been known as the Holy Ground their head-quarters. Some time in December, Gen. Claiborne, piloted by Sam Moniac and an old McGillivray negro, got near the place before the Indians discovered them. The Indians began to cross their wives and children over the river; they had scarcely time to do that before the army arrived—a skirmish ensued, and the Indians, losing a few men, gave way in every directoon. Weatherford was among the last to quit the place. He made an attempt to go down the river —that is, down the bank of the river—but found that the soldiers would intercept his passage, and he turned up, keeping on the bluff near the river, until he reached the ravine or little branch that makes into the river above where the town used to be. There was a small foot-path that crossed the ravine near the river; he carried his horse down that path, and instead of going out of the ravine at the usual crossing, he kept up it towards its head, until he passed the lines of the whites. So, now you have the bluff-jumping story.

This story was told long before Weatherford died. Maj. Cowles and myself asked him how that report got out. He said Sam Moniac knew him, and seeing him on horse back on the brink of the bluff, and his diappearing so suddenly, caused those who saw him to believe that he had gone over the bluff. He said that he ran a greater risk in going the way he did, than he would to have gone over the bluff; and but for his horse he would have gone over it and crossed the river. But it was to save his pony that he risked 'passing between two lines of the whites. From that circumstance the report got out, and he would often own to it for the gratification of some, as they wanted to be deceived any how. But in going the way he did, it was hazarding more than one in a thousand would do, for a hundred times the value of a pony.

There was one Indian, if no more, killed at Holy Ground. I believe it from this circumstance. Some years after the fight, and the whites began to settle Alabama, a very poor man by the name of Stoker settled on the Autauga side, and opposite Holy Ground. His little boys, while out hunting one day, found the irons of an old trunk and some $150 or $200 in eagle half dollars; this, I have no doubt, was plundered at Fort Mims, and the plunderer placed it where the boys of Stoker found it, and went back into the fight at Holy Ground and was killed.

Weatherford said that after he escaped from the Holy Ground, he began to think over what was next to be done; the Indians were without ammunition, but little to eat, armies marching in from all quarters; the Spaniards at Pensacola seemed afraid to aid them, as they had done at the commencement—everything seemed to forbode the destruction of him and his people. He fell in with Savannah or Sowanoka Jack, and they consulted together as to what was best. Jack proposed to get as many of their people as they could; that in a few years the whites would entirely surround them; the Spaniards in Florida would afford them no protection. They then agreed to watch the movements of the Georgia army, to see if there could be no chance to get ammunition. They did so; and waited until Gen. Floyd camped near Calebee. They had collected the largest number of warriors that had been collected during the war. They saw that Gen.

Floyd intended crossing the creek, from his quitting the Tuckabatchy route. The night before the fight, which commenced before day, the Indians camped near what was called McGarth's still-house branch, on the west side of the branch, and held a council. He proposed to wait until the army started to cross the creek, and as the advanced guard reached the hill on the next side, the fire on the guard should be the signal for the attack; that the army was small, and could be attacked on all sides; and that they would at least stand a chance to get hold of the ammunition, if they did not defeat the whites. But to attack the whites in their camp, who were well supplied with ammunition and five pieces of cannon, would be folly, unless the Indians had more ammunition. The chiefs overruled him, and he, with a few Tuskegees, quit the camp and started back, and when he reached Pole-Cat Springs he heard the firing commence. It is my belief that had Weatherford's advice been taken, the result of that affair would have been very different; for long before the fight closed, I could understand Indian enough to hear them asking each other to "give me some bullets—give me powder." The friendly Indians with us did us no good, except Timpoochy Barnard and his Uchees. Jim Boy and Billy McDonald, or Billy McGillivray, as he was best known, said that they had between 1800 and 2000 men; but many of them were without guns, and only had war-clubs and bows and arrows.

The surrender of Weatherford to Gen. Jackson you have had from various sources—you must judge who you think most correct. I have heard Gen. Jackson say that if he was capable of forming anything like a correct judgment of a man on a short acquaintance, that he pronounced Weatherford to be as high-toned and fearless as any man he had met with—one whose very nature scorned a mean action. And Gen. Jackson's treatment to Billy Weatherford proved that he believed what he said; for, had Weatherford proved any other than Jackson took him to be, he would have met the fate of Francis and Nehemarthla-Micco.

What I have here written is as correct as my memory will allow, for I have no history to refer to.

Yours, &c.,
T. S. W.

————

WHEELING, WINN PARISH LA. ⎱
Nov. 3, 1858. ⎰

J. J. HOOPER, ESQ.:

Dear Sir: A day or two since I sent you some sketches of the life of Billy Weatherford, in which I forgot to say that he never was in the hearing of the fire of a gun during the Creek war, except at Fort Mims, Holy Ground, and Floyd's battle at Calebee Creek, and only heard the firing at Calebee from Polè-Cat Springs.

In a letter addressed to me through the Mail, by Col. Pickett, in February last, he says that himself and I are as well acquainted with the modern Creek Indians, perhaps, as any two persons living. That may be so; but I think there is this difference between us: his information has been derived from very vague testimony, and gathered up at too late a date to form anything like a true or correct history; and, unfortunately for me, too much of mine has been from personal experience and from the most authentic testimony, and at an early day. It is true, that one so capable of writing as the Colonel could have given the world not only a tolerably true, but quite an interesting history.

I see that the Colonel, like many others, is inclined to hold out an idea or belief that the American Indian descended from the Jew; and from what I am now about to write, should it ever come under his notice, he may think that I am somewhat of an Indian genealogist; but by no means would I have him think that I am a descendant of the Jew, or write from or by inspiration. Now, had I known in 1836, when I saw the Col. in Walker's old store house in Tuskegee, that he intended writing a history of the Creek Indians, I would at least have offered him as much assistance as Gen. Jackson in 1830 offered the Congress of the United States in aiding it to establish a United States Bank. I would most cheerfully have furnished him with facts which would have enabled him to write a very fair history. And I will go farther than Gen. Jackson did—I will prove that I was capable of performing what I might have promised. I will commence with the several Indian Agents from 1790 down to 1832, give their names, the names of their children, and then the names of the most noted Indian countrymen and their children, with the names of many half breeds and full bloods and their children.

James Seagrove, an Irishman, was first Agent. His white family I never knew; he had a half breed son, who was killed by the Indians many years ago for killing another Indian at Kiemulga, when the first McIntosh party were emigrating to Arkansas territory.

Col. Ben. Hawkins, a native of Warren county, N. C., was next Agent. He raised three daughters—Georgia, Carolina and Virginia—and one son, James Madison, called after the Col.'s class-mate in college, who was afterwards President of the United States. Col. Hawkins raised a girl who was called by the name of Muscogee Hawkins. She was the daughter of John Hill, who was a sub-Indian Agent. He hung himself at Fort Wilkinson many years ago. Muscogee married Capt. Kit Kizer, of the U. S. Army; he died, and she married Bagwell Tillor; but enough of her. Georgia died at about twenty years of age with consumption, a most beautiful and amiable girl. One of the younger girls married a Lieutenant Loshsha of the army. The other daughter and Madison I lost sight of, as I left the country a great while back; but they were all handsome and intelligent children. Col. Hawkins died in the fall of 1816, and sleeps on the East bank of Flint river, and none are left who know the spot where he rests but myself and, perchance, some old Indian countrymen.

The next Agent was Gen. David Brady Mitchell, a very talented Scotchman. His oldest son, William, a man of fine sense and well educated, married Jane McIntosh; the second son, David B., married a Miss Thweatt. He was quite a gentleman; he died while a young man. The two younger sons, John and Bullock, I have not seen for more than forty years. The oldest daughter, Sarah, a most splendid woman, married a Col. McClung, of North Alabama. The youngest daughter, Mary, (or Button, as she was sometimes called,) was like her sister; she married Gen. Wm. Taylor.

The next Agent was my old and intimate friend, Col. John Crowell. Many, both white and red, yet live who have shared his kind hopitalities. He sleeps upon Fort Mitchell Hill, where rest a crowd that no one need be ashamed to be picked up with, in a coming day.

One of the first Indian traders was George Galphin, an Irishman. He raised a large family; and of the five varieties of the human family; he raised children from three, and no doubt would have gone the whole hog, but the Malay and Mongrel were out of his reach. His white children were of the highest and most polished order—Mrs. Governor Milledge was one of them. He had two negroes, Mina, a woman, and Ketch, a man; they were brother and sister. He raised one daughter from Mina, and called her Barbary. She married an Irishman by the name of Holmes, and raised Dr. Thomas G. Holmes, whom Col. Pickett often alludes to in his History of Alabama, as having had conversations with him. At Galphin's death Mina was set free, and died at old Timothy Barnard's, on Flint river, Ga., many years back. Ketch was an interpreter among the Indians for Galphin—was his stock minder—kept stock at Galphin's cowpens, where Louisville in Jefferson coounty, Ga., now stands, and which was once the seat of government of that State. Ketch helped to put up the first cabin at old Galphinton,

on the Ogeechee, for an Indian trading house. At Galphin's death Ketch was sold, and was purchased by Gen.
Twiggs of the revolution. He was the body servant of
Gen. Twiggs during the war. At the close of the war,
Ketch left his master and went into the Creek Natiion.
In 1833 the present Gen. Twiggs, who has performed more
real, active and hard service (such as required great bodily
exertion as well as great courage) than any one man living—I cannot even except the greatest military man of
this or any other age, the veteran Scott—when severe
bodily exertion has been called for. There is scarcely an
Indian tribe on our borders that Gen. Twiggs has not had
to war with, or deal with, in some way or other; and in
addition to this, the battles of Palo Alto, Resaca de la
Palma, Monterey, Vera Cruz, Cerro Gordo, and every
other battle field in Mexico, speak the praise of Twiggs,
Quitman, Worth and others. Gen. Twiggs gave Ketch
to me. He [Ketch] was about six feet six inches high,
very straight, and retained his bodily strength as well as
mental faculties, to a most astonishing degree. The Gen.
did not give me Ketch expecting me to profit by it, but
wished him cared for in his old age, as he had been a faithful
servant to his father in trying times. I purchased Ketch's
family, and he lived till 1840. I buried him under a large
oak about a mile from Tuskegee, a place that he had selected for that purpose. I had a little mill on a creek near
Tuskegee, where I kept Ketch and several other Indian
negroes, and here I used to spend much time in listening
to them tell over old occurrences of by-gone days. From
the best calculation we could make, Ketch lived to be
near a hundred years old.

While I am sketching off a little negro history, I will
mention one or two others. I buried Barnard's old Kitty
near Tuskegee, at a time when Amy, her youngest daughter of nine children, had great grand children. Old Kitty
was an African by birth, and could give no account of her
age; but she was a very old woman, at least to live since
Noah's time. Another, and the most remarkable negro

that I have known in my time, was Polly Perryman, by many known as Chehaw Micco Polly. She was raised by an English family at Nassau on the Island of New Providence. She was taken to Mobile when about grown— that was but a short time after the French evacuated Fort Du Quesne, or Pittsburg. I have often heard her tell of making the acquaintance of some Virginia negroes who were with the French. Polly was sold to one Jas. Clark, and taken to Pensacola. Clark sold her to an old Indian countryman by the name of Theophilus Perryman, who was the father of the old half breed, Jim Perryman, of the Octiyokny town; and Jim was the father of as many children as Priam. These were the Chattahoochy Indians below Fort Gaines. Polly was then sold to Lauchlan McGillivray, and taken to the Coosa river a short distance below Proctor's Island, at the old Bob Cornells place, known by some as Little Tallasse—named after Bob's wife, who was a Tallasse, and the mother of Alexander Cornells, the U. S. interpreter. Polly lived in the McGillivray family when Sophia and Alexander were born. She lived with Alexander after he was grown, and after his death Billy Panthon sold her to the half breed, Jim Perryman, and he sold her to Chehaw-Micco.

When the Indians emigrated in 1836, she and old Rose were left with me, and I carried them to Arkansas. Polly was the mother of the celebrated Siro, who was supposed to have been killed in the Pea River fight in 1837. Polly died in 1846, and said she was 115 years old; and I think she was but little short of that. She was as intelligent as negroes ever get to be.

I purchased Holmes' old Ned from "Horse Shoe Ned."* He had been raised at an early day by a family of Powells, one of whom was the father of Hossa Yoholo, a reckless fighter of the old war. Ned followed this chief to Florida, where he died on Indian river, from a disease in his feet, caused by an insect known as the jigger. And from this, Hossa Yoholo, and the ignorance of many, Us-

---

*Mr. Edward Hanrick, of Montgomery.—II.

sa Yoholo, or Black Drink, the modern Oceola, derived much of his fame. · Horse Shoe will tell you that Ned was an intelligent negro.

The ignorant and unobserving will laugh, no doubt, at my introducing negro testimony in relation to history; but I have gathered much interesting information from those negroes, as well as McGillivray's old Charles, who accompanied his old master to Savannah, Ga. The old man McGillivray never returned to the Nation, but sent his two children, Sophia and Aleck, back by Charles. This I think I stated to you before. But let me here remark one thing about negroes—particularly negroes who are raised in the slaveholding States of the United States. They are in general treated kind, and in early life are placed pretty much on an equality with the white children. They have but few cares, and what they learn they generally learn well; and they never fail to learn all the family names. You may take any old negro who has lived for three or four generations in a family, and nine out of ten will tell you the names of the oldest down to the youngest for several generations. For the want of a paper record, they register these things in their heads. The recollection of family names for a few generations back is a thing which a very large portion of the American people are deficient in. Indian negroes generally have a double advantage in the recollection of things, if not of names, over those raised among the whites. They are raised to man or womanhood with their owners; and in many instances they are better raised—always on an equality, and not one in fifty but speaks the English as well as the Indian language. Nearly all of them, at some time or other, are used as interpreters, which affords them an opportunity to gather information that many of their owners never have, as they speak but the one language.

I have said enough on this subject, if I am right, to satisfy sensible men; and if wrong, more than they perhaps would like to read—and as I have no marvellous yarns to relate, or pictures in my work, fools won't look at it.

Now, let us go back to family names—maybe some one will want to write hereafter, and I will furnish them at least a few names of persons who have, and are yet living. Timothy Barnard, an Englishman, was a trader and interpreter for many years. I knew him well—he had an Uchee woman for a wife, and raised a number of children. Jim was his oldest son, and a cripple through life; Billy was the next, and married Peggy Sullivan, a daughter of Sullivan who was the owner of the negro Bob that was said to be concerned in the murder of the Kirkland family at Murder creek, from which the creek took its name. Bob was the father of Cæsar, who was with Gen. Dale in the canoe fight. The mother of Cæsar was old Tabby, who was stolen from a man by the name of Cook in Georgia many years back. Billy's and Peggy's children were Davy, Tom, Epsy, Nancy and Sukey. Timpoochy, the third son, had an Indian wife; he commanded the Uchees in Gen. Floyd's night fight, and was as lion-hearted as Gen. Zachary Taylor. Cuseene, the fourth son, had an Indian wife, and emigrated to Arkansas; Michy, the fifth son, a fine soldier, got drunk one night at his camp and was burned to death; Buck, the youngest, was a smart half breed; he packed horses for me while I was assisting Gen. Watson in running the line between Georgia and Florida; he was murdered not far from Sand Fort by an Indian. Polly, his oldest daughter, married Joe Marshall. She was killed by a horse. The only son she had by Marshall was John, who commanded the five Indians that burned the last stages and killed Hammel and Lucky in Russell county, in 1836. The next daughter was Matoya, a very pretty woman; she died single, but was courted by Daniel McGee, of old Hartford, Ga.

The next important trader was Laughlin McGillivray. I have given you an account of him before. Daniel McDonald, who was the principal pack-horse man for McGillivray, assumed the name of Daniel McGillivray, and got considerable property by it. McDonald was the fa-

ther of Bit-nose Billy McGillivray, as he has been called
and known by many.

James McQueen was the first white man I ever heard
of being among the Creeks. He was born in 1683—went
into the Nation in 1716, and died in 1811. He married a
Tallassee woman. The Tallassees then occupied a portion of Talladega county. In 1756 he moved the Tallassees down opposite Tuckabatchy, and settled the Netches
under the chief Chenubby and Dixon Moniac, a Hollander, who was the father of Sam Moniac, at the Tallassee
old fields, on the Tallasahatchy creek. McQueen settled
himself on Line creek, in Montgomery county. I knew
several of his childred—that is, his sons, Bob, Fullunny
and Peter. Bob was a very old man when I first knew
him. He and Fullunny had Indian wives. Peter, the
youngest son, married Betsy Durant. They raised one
son, James, and three daughters, Milly, Nancy and Tallassee. The Big Warrior's son, Yargee, had the three
sisters for wives at the same time, and would have taken
more half sisters. After Peter McQueen died, his widow
returned from Florida and married Willy McQueen, the
nephew of Peter, and raised two daughters, Sophia and
Muscogee, and some two or three boys. Old James Mc-
Queen had a daughter named Ann, commonly called Nancy. He called her after the Queen of England, whose
service he quit when he came into the Nation. Of late
years it was hard to find a young Tallassee without some
of the McQueen blood in his veins.

This daughter, Ann, raised a daughter by one Copinger,
and called her Polly. She was the mother of Ussa Yoholo, or Black drink—but better known of late as Oceola—
who aided in the murder of my old countyman, General
Thompson. And for the capture of Oceola, Gen. Thomas
S. Jessup deserves as much credit as Peter Francisco would,
had he flogged his grand-mother. Oceola, as he was called,
was born in Macon county, on the East side of Nafawpba*
creek, and not far from where the West Point Railroad

*Now known as Euphaubee.

crosses. If I ever return to Alabama, I will mark the spot for some one. His great grand-father, James McQueen, lies about a mile off, and on the West side of the creek.

The next traders I will introduce are Joe and Bob Cornells. Joe had a Tuckabatchy woman for a wife. They raised three sons, Davy, George and James. Davy was the oldest; he was known to the Indians as the Dog Warrior, or Efaw Tustanugga. He was the father of the present speaker of the Upper Creeks, Hopoithle Yoholo, and another son, Miker. He [Davy Cornell] was a troublesome man, and was killed by one Harrison, while on a visit to Seagrove at Colerain, bearing a white flag.

George, the second son, raised two sons, Seechy and Dick. Seechy raised several chidren, sons and daughters; his daughter, Tomger, married a Mr. Spire M. Hagerty,* and he fell heir to her property. Dick had several wives. He raised one daughter by his second cousin, Sukey Cornells, named Hannah.

A man named Sam Jones took with him into the Nation from Fort Wilkinson a woman named Betsy Coulter; Jim Cornells swapped his niece, Polly Kean, with Jones, and took Betsy Coulter for a wife. She was the woman that Peter McQueen and Jim Boy captured and carried to Pensacola, and sold to Madame Barrone. Sam Jones married Polly Kean—and in 1816, and near about the time that Col. Fisher and Jim Collier killed Bradberry, and Col. Joe Phillips killed Roberts, Jim Cornells killed Sam Jones. Polly then married one-eyed Billy Oliver, an old countyman of mine. She was the daughter of Lucy Cornells, who as the daughter of old Joe. Her first husband was John Kean; she raised Polly, whom I have just mentioned, and one son, John. Kean died, and she married one Sam Smith, and raised one son, who was called Sam. He was wounded at Fort Mims, and made his escape. Old Smith quit Lucy, and she then married one Tooly. He was a blacksmith, and worked up the little

*Who put her away, after removing to Red River, and took for wife a widow Hawkins.—H.

swivel into bells which DeSoto left at Thlea Walla. Lucy had two daughters by Tooly, Judy and Mahaly; they
were entirely too ugly to think of marrying. Tooly had
two sons, Billy and Hiram; they went off among the
whites. One of the Crawfords in Georgia partly raised
Hiram; he returned to the Nation, and was killed by Pom-
pey, a negro.

Vicey Cornells, the second daughter of Joe Cornells,
married Alexander McGillivray; and after he died, she
married Zach McGirth, and raised several daughters—one
married Vardy Jolly, one Ned James, one Aleck Moniac,
one Bill Crabtree, and the youngest, Sarah, went to Ar
kansas.

I could give you more of this, but you live too near
Montgomery to know it all.

Mrs. McGirth raised one son, called James, who was
killed at Fort Mims, and she and her daughters were saved
by Jim Boy. I lived long with them both; often have I
heard them talk it over, when both were sure to get drunk,
if whisky could be had.

George Cornells, the son of Joe, raised several daughters; the old Mad-Dog's son married one of them, and
was the father of Capt. Walker's wife, Sappoya, and a
boy, the great friend to Horse Shoe Ned, called Mungy.
The young Dog Warrior was killed at Otisee in 1813.
Col. Pickett calls him the Mad Dragon. Another of
George's daughters married Billy McGirth; another the
Little Doctor, and one called Big Lizzy married Mad Blue
Bob Cornells, the brother of old Joe. I have mentioned
in the sketches of Polly Perryman, the negress, that he
was the father of Alexander Cornells, the interpreter.
Alexander Cornells' wife was known as the Big Woman.
She was the daughter of the old Mad-Dog by the mother
of Tuskenea. The stock was good.

The Big Woman's first daughter, Anny, was not a Cornells; her father was Tom Low. Sukey was Alexander's
first child by the Big Woman; she had her second cousin,
Dick Cornells, for a husband. Charles was their oldest

son, who hung himself in 1827 or 28. He had Peggy Mc-
Gillivray for a wife, the daughter of Alexander McGillivray.

Hawkins Cornells' wife was an Indian. He and Charles
left several children. But long before Charles hung himself, his wife, Peggy McGillivray, died, and he married the
widow of Bob Mosely; her name was Sumerly. She was
a grand-daughter of old Sim McQueen. Bob Mosely was
a white man, whom I mentioned to you before, in connection with John Ward.

Anny Low, the oldest daughter of Alexander Cornells'
wife, had George Goodwin for a husband. Goodwin was
the half brother of Jim Boy, and the man we picked up,
with a few others, when we went to Moniac's cowpens in
company with Weatherford, a few days after his surrender
to Gen. Jackson.

The next is Ben or Peter Durant—he was called by both
names—who was a South Carolinian of French origin.
He came to the Nation and married Sophia McGillivray,
sister of Alexander. They raised three sons, Laughlin,
John and Sandy. Laughlin married a Miss Hall, who
was born and raised at or near the Cow-ford on St. Johns
river, East Florida, where Jacksonville is now. John and
Sandy went off with Peter McQueen to Florida. After
the old Creek war, Sandy died at Tampa Bay; John went
to the Island of New Providence. Laughlin Durant
raised severel children. His daughter, Sarah, brought up
pretty much by Davy White in Mobile, married Sam Adams, who once run a line of stages from Vera Cruz to the
city of Mexico, and afterwards run a line through the
Creek Nation, and was with Jim Greene the night he was
killed and the first stages were burned.

The daughters of Ben Durant were Rachel, who married Billy McGirth, a son of Daniel McGirth, of revolutionary memory; they raised one son, named Billy. After McGirth's death, she married Davy Walker, and raised
two sons, Davy and Ben; after Walker died, she married
a man by the name of Bershius, and was living among

the Choctaws the last I knew of her. Polly, the second
daughter, married a full blooded Tallassee, named Cochir-
ny, and lived like all other Indians. Sophia married a
Dr. Macomes; Betsy married Peter McQueen, which I
have already mentioned.

The McIntosh family is next. It has been a matter of
dispute with some as to the name of the father of Billy
and Rolin McIntosh—whether it was Rolin or Lauchlan;
but I think it was the latter, for I knew a half brother of
Billy and Rolin who was a full white man. He was in
the Legislature of Georgia, and I think he told me his
father was Lauchlan McIntosh. Billy and Rolin were half
brothers. Billy was the greatest man I ever knew to have
been raised entirely among the Indians. His history is
well known; but I will give you the names of some of
his children. His oldest daughter, by a Creek woman,
was named Jane. She married Billy Mitchell, a son of
the then Agent; after that she married Sam Hawkins,
who was killed at the same time McIntosh was. She then
married Paddy Carr, but left him and moved to Arkansas at an early day. His [McIntosh's] other Creek children were Chilly and Lewis, sons, and Hetty and Lucy,
daughters. His daughter by the Cherokee woman married Ben Hawkins, the brother of Sam. Ben was killed
many years ago in Texas, and at the time Hopoithle Yoholo's son, called Dick Johnson, was killed. Ben Hawkins' widow married Spire M. Hagarty, who before that
had the daughter of Seechy Cornells for a wife. Billy had
a half brother on the mother's side, named Hagy. He
was often called a McIntosh, but was a full Indian. Rolin is now the principal chief of the lower towns—an
honest, good man, and as brave as men ever get to be.

The next are the Marshalls. Old man Marshall was an
Englishman. He settled where Columbus, Ga., now is.
He had three sons, Joe, Jim and Ben. Joe was a true
friend to the whites, and so were his brothers. He was a
good fighter, and lost one of his eyes defending the Tuckabatchys, when they were forted in, in time of the war.

He was killed by a drunken Indian after the whites settled the country in Chambers county. Jim, I think, died in Russell county, Ala.; and Ben, a very intelligent man, is yet living in Arkansas.

To go through with the Derrysaws, Steadhams, Howards, Linders, Hollingers, McGees, Hawkins', Graysons, Bruners, Keeners, Danileys, Lotts, Baileys, Fishers, Birfords, Brintons, Reeds, Gregorys, Hales, Rileys, and a great many other whites and half breeds whom I have known and could name, would be too tedious, and would be coming up in the neighborhood of John's views, as to the sayings and doingsof his master during a three years' service. The world, no doubt, would hold my books, but they would at least be too lengthy for newspaper publication. So, I will give you an account of the Riley family, and then go on with the full Indians.

John O'Riley, more generally known as pacing John Riley, was an Irishman; he had two half breed sons by a Tuskegee woman, Barney and John. Barney, at the commencement of the old Creek war, was hostile; but after the skirmish at the old Tuckabatchy Town, he joined the whites, and was Gen. Floyd's principal pilot. He was a daring man, very high tempered and easily irritated. He rendered much service to the whites. I volunteered one night to go with a Capt. Harvey, of Jefferson county, Ga., on a scount from Fort Hall. Barney was our pilot; we were on horse back; I had taken the place of a sick dragoon, is the reason why I was on horse back. We crossed Line creek late in the night, and about a mile up Milly's creek from the old Federal road, we found some Indians; we killed two men and took Bob Mosely's wife and children. After the war and Alabama was settled by the whites, John Lucas employed Barney to go with him to the Western District of Tennessee. On their route back, Barney got drunk; Lucas struck him with a stick, (so Barney said;) Barney killed Lucas; took his horse and some other things, and brought them to Alabama and told what he had done. He was tried by the Indians for the

offence, and was condemned and shot near the road, on
the East side of Line creek. John Riley was also a fine
soldier; I had him with me in Florida in 1818. If living,
he is in Arkansas.

The next is the Big Warrior, the largest man I ever saw
among the Creeks. He was almost as spotted as a Leop-
ard. He was a Tuckabatchy, and the ranking chief in
the Nation, and the principal chief of the Upper Towns.
The Big Warrior was a descendant of the Hopungiesas,
or Piankeshaws, as the whites call them. These people
emigrated from New Mexico to the waters of the Ohio
about a hundred years after the Muscogees left the Gulf
coast, and settled Alabama and a portion of Georgia. Big
Warrior used to boast much of his Northern blood and
ancestry; and that circumstance gave rise to the blunders
of Col. Pickett and Mr. Compeer, about the Tuckabatchys
being a Northern tribe and coming to the country after
the Tallassees and others had settled it. Big Warrior was
a man of great cunning, and there is but little sincerity
in his pretended friendship for the whites. He was the
father of Tuskenea, who was a much better man. Tuskenea's mother and the Big Woman's mother was the
same woman. Old Mad-Dog, who in his time held the
same rank as the Big Warrior, was the father of the Big
Woman, and Big Warrior was the father of Tuskenea.
A brother of Tuskenea's mother, the oldest man I ever
saw, fought with the French against Braddock. James
McQueen sent him with a party of Creeks to war with
the English.

In the revolution there never was a Tallassee or a Netches known to take up arms against the colonies; that was
the influence of McQueen and Dick Moniac, the Hollander. Nat Collins and myself located this old Indian upon
his land; I forget his Indian name, but he was called Billy by the whites. He died in 1836.

Col. Pickett speaks of knowing Menauway, the leader
at Horse Shoe. The Colonel or myself one is mistaken.
I have known Menauway since 1809; the first time that

I ever saw him was at Booth's Indian store, on the Ocmulga, in 1809 ; he was there in company with Sam Dale and Harrison Young, the brother of Simon Suggs. I recollect that Young and Menauway were just getting over the small pox ; they had both had the disease at Menauway's house at Ocfuskee. It was at that time that Dale and Webb laid the foundation for the fist fight at Clinton, which I was telling you about.

Menauway told me the way he escaped at Horse Shoe. He was badly wounded, and discovered that the whites and friendly Indians paid but little attention to dead women ; he got some women's clothes, put them on, dragged two or three dead women together, and lay between them until night, and then escaped. I reckon the cow story was like the hog-skin at Talladega—all a hoax.

The Colonel says hundreds of Indians used to visit his father's store. He is mistaken ; there were some Indians, but many of them were white men from Col. Rose's neighborhood, Matthew Duncan, and others. I knew the place long before the Colonel's father settled it, and long after ; he sold it to that miser, John Crayon ; but he could not help being a miser.

I will send you some Georgia and S. Carolina sketches before long, nd you can then account for Crayon's being a miser. Respectfully,

T. S. W.

———

WHEELING WINN PARISH, LA., }
November 27th, 1858. }

To J. J. HOOPER, Esq:

Dear Sir :—My health has been bad of late—so much so, that I have been unable to write. I sent you a few days back a little document containing some corrections of errors in my printed letters. You will find that in the hand-writing of my son Thomas, and I believe without date.

8

Your paper makes its appearance occasionally, and I find many good things in it, besides much useful information. But I am truly sorry to find it the messenger of so much sad intelligence. I learn from it, that my old acquantances, (and I think they were my friends,) Col. A. J. Pickett, Ex-Governor Bagby, and Col. Charles McLemore are no more.

Col. Pickett I knew when a small boy, at the time when his father emigrated to Alabama, I think in 1818. I was then in the prime of manhood. Col. Wm. R. Pickett settled in Autauga county, near Hayne's Bluff—the bluff taking its name from its original owner, Col. Arthur P. Hayne. That portion of country between Autauga creek and the mouth of Coosa river, just before, and at the time, and a little while after Col. Wm. R. Pickett settled in Alabama, was occupied by more intelligent, sensible, practical, and I may say talented men, (not to be professional men,) than any portion of South Alabama which I was acquainted with. Among them was Dr. Bibb, the first man I ever heard make a political speech. I think it was in 1804, at Elbert Court House, Ga.. I was too young to understand anything of politics at that time; but I remember hearing the speech and recollect the man, and knew him from then until his death. I also recollect that at the same time Bibb's step-father, William Barnett, made a short speech. They were both Senators in Congress after that, and I think at the same time.

Boling Hall was one among many other intelligent men who settled in Autauga county at an early day.

There was also Phillips Fitzpatrick, one of the earliest settlers of Autauga; and if being raised on the frontiers of Georgia at an early day had deprived him of an education, he was certainly under as many obligations to his maker for native intellect as any man I have known, living or dead.

You will discover from what I have written, that I differ from Col. A. J. Pickett in some things relative to the early history of Alabama, and more particularly that of the

Creek Indians. Notwithstanding I have differed from
him as to history, I agree with all who knew him, that he
was a high-toned gentleman, and his loss is much to be
lamented. Col. Pickett possessed to a great degree a trait
that is seldom, if ever, possessed by any any but the best
of men—that is, too great confidence in the honesty of
mankind. That no doubt has been the cause of some
things appearing in his history which a few of us old ones
know to be incorrect. He has lived to inform himself,
and to instruct his fellow man, and never (as I have heard)
engaged in the political broils and troubles that have agi-
tated the country in his time. That of itself is enough
to make his memory revered by all who knew him.

My acquaintance with Governor Bagby commenced, I
think, in 1819. In that year and the year after, I had
business that called me to Claiborne frequently, and on
one of my stays at that place, I was introduced to Mr.
Bagby by a lady adquaintance of mine, a Miss Emily Steel.
She afterwards married Mr. Bagby. In June, 1820, I, in
company with an Englishman by the name of William N.
Thompson, visited Claiborne. Thompson was going to
Mobile on horse-back, and I remained at Claiborne until
he returned; I spent much of that time in company with
Governor Bagby. About the time Thompson returned to
Claiborne, a steamboat called the Cotton Plant, I think,
made its appearance at the lower landing. The Captain
gave a general invitation to the citizens of Claiborne to
attend a party on board the boat. I, with many others,
both male and female, attended the party. We danced
on the hurricane deck. The fiddler was one Tom Paxton,
who played for me when I taught the first dancing school
that was ever taught in Montgomery county. It was at
the house of one Isaac Lansdale, near the mouth of Catoma creek. Capt. John Martin was one of my pupils.
The party closed on the boat,.and all hands returned to
town. I put up at a house kept by John M. Flynn. Gen.
Sam Dale was my room-mate. The Englishman, Thompson, also boarded with Flynn. Bagby boarded at a house

kept by three brothers, all gamblers—John, Henry, and
Robert Carter. Bagby invited Dale, Thompson, and myself to supper at the Carter house one night. After supper, it was proposed to have some speaking or debating on
the propriety of Congress calling Gen. Jackson's conduct
in question for his march into Florida a year or two before
that. One Laurence Wood was called to the Chair, and
Bagby made the first speech, one of the finest I think I
ever heard from so young a man, or I may say boy—for
he was not grown, and wore a very boyish appearance.
There was one James Pickens who made the next speech.
He took the same ground that Bagby had taken pretty
much; justifying Gen. Jackson's course, under the circumstances; and also contended that our relations with
Spain made it necessary for Congress to do something, or
at least say something, in order to appease Spain. Bagby
seemed well pleased with Pickens' speech, which was de-
livered in fine style, and showed much good sense on the
part of the speaker.

The next thing in order was to drink some liquor, and
while drinking, a man by the name of Burwell Brewer
made some uncalled for, as well as unbecoming remarks
about Henry Clay , of Kentucky, and Tom Cobb, of Ga.
Brewer's remarks offended Bagby, he [Bagby] being a
great admirer of Mr. Clay.   He swore the speaking should
stop, and mounted upon the speaker's or chairman's table
with a decanter in one hand and a tumbler in the other ;
he was ordered down, but he threw the decanter at one
man and the tumbler at another, and a fight ensued in
which Bagby seemed to have but few friends.   I, with the
leg of a small table, succeeded in warding off several severe blows that Bagby would have received, as well as cuts
from knives, which were made at him.   Dale, who was
out when the fight commenced, hearing the noise, ran in,
in company with three others, Flynn, Reading and Hail-
stock.   With their assistance we got Bagby out of the
house, and carried him to Flynn's.

By some means, or from some cause, angry words passed

between Flynn and Reading, and not long after that, Reading killed Flynn. But for the very determined resolution of Dale, I think Bagby would have been killed that night; for there were some very determined men among those who were opposed to him—among them, I understood, was the man Pickens above alluded to. He was a stranger to me; but I learned he would not give an insult, nor was he ever known to receive one and let it go unpunished.

Ever after that, when I met with Arthur P. Bagby, he would express great friendship for me. While the seat of government was kept at Cahawba, I resided near Selma; and during one session of the Legislature, the Englishman, Thompson, called at my house and I accompanied him to Cahawba. While there, we met with Bagby; he invited us to his room, whish was at Davy White's hotel. On our entering, the room, we met with Sam Dale, Nick Davis, from Limestone, James Jackson, from Lauderdale, Matt Clay, I think from Madison, Phil. Fitzpatrick, from Autauga, Jew Davis, from Mobile, better known as "the original George." Liquor, anecdotes, songs and loud laughter went round until late at night—all hands as happy as they would have been at a camp-meeting. The show was about closing, and all in fine spirits and the best of humors, when Phil. Fitzpatrick unfortunately wanted a little more fun, and whispered to Dale that he did not understand some remarks which had been made by some of the gentlemen present, and that he [Dale] ought to have the matter explained; and for all Dale had known Phil. from his childhood, and had witnessed many of his tricks, there was too much liquor aboard for good judgment to have its sway. Dale rose up, closed the door, and swore no man should leave the room until an explanation was made, and that it should be made very promptly, or he would frail the last man in the room. The rest being pretty much in Dale's fix, did not know what to say. Clay said that he would quit the room; Dale stood at the door and demanded an explanation; from that their

coats were thrown off, and we were about to have another
Claiborne affair of it, when Phil. spoke to Dale and told
him that he had fallen on a plan to have the matter settled, and that he [Dale] had more courage than any one
of the crowd, and was obliged to quit winner. That satisfied Dale, and the show closed. The next morning it
was like an Indian quarrel—all charged to whisky.

For the last eight or ten years of my stay in Alabama,
I do not recollect to have seen Gov. Bagby but once. In
June, 1840, I had a son at school in Tuscaloosa, and there
was to be a Whig covention there. I concluded to visit
both; and on my route to Tuscaloosa, at a place in Autauga county, I fell in with the Englishman, Thompson,—
and here let me remark, that he was a man of fine intelligence. I had then known him twenty years; our first
acquaintance was near a place then known as Dardenoil,
now called by many Dardanell; it is in Arkansas. He
and myself traveled together to Tuscaloosa. My health
was not good, and on my arrival at Tuscaloosa I found
my son sick; so, I could not hear all the speaking. But
on the day that Judge Hopkins was to speak, I, with
my friend Thompson, went to the log cabin. Hopkins
spoke. I heard many speeches in 1840, made by good
speakers; I heard Mr. Hilliard in his best days; I heard
Dixon H. Lewis, at Clayton, in Barbour county; I heard
Judge Berrien and Mr. Preston, at Macon, Ga., besides
hundreds of the little short stock, who deal alone on borrowed capital, and are often very profuse with it; but
none did I hear that surpassed Judge Hopkins, if, indeed,
any equalled him. If there could have been the smallest
particle of modesty squeezed into the most noisy dema-
gogue, and he forced to have heard that speech, he would
have hung his head at hearing so many truths, and they
uttered in a manner that the most common capacity could
understand them and know their importance.

After the Judge closed, and Mr. Morrisett, from Monroe county,—who had been a soldier under Gen. Harrison—made a few remarks, Thompson and myself left for

our rooms. On our way, in front of Duffie's hotel, some one called me; I turned, and found it was Gov. Bagby. He seemed glad to see me, and remarked—"You and the Englishman still travel together; now, if you had Dale, the crowd would be complete." He then asked me if I was a Whig. I answered him, "if there was a better one on earth than myself, it was only because he had more sense." He then made the same inquiry of Thompson, if he was a Whig. Thompson said he was. The Governor then asked us if we were not wrong. I replied to him, "Governor, you perhaps can judge better of that yourself, as you have been on all sides." He reddened a little in the face, and remarked to Thomson: "You know, Thompson, that Tom Woodward and Sam Dale are privileged men with me."

That was the last time I ever saw Governor Bagby. He was a man of fine sense and good heart. It was often said of him, that he was a bad manager in money matters, and did not accumulate wealth. But he could have done so, no doubt, had he wished it at any time; though, like a man of sense, he chose to live well on what he made, and never, like many others, cared to have large sums lying by him, merely to hear fools say that he had it. Vacancies which occur by the death of such men as Arthur P. Bagby, are not so easily filled in Alabama or elsewhere, in the present day; and the people of Alabama, as well as many other States, seem to have foreknown this for some time back, and have accustomed themselves to putting men of much less calibre in the highest places. Like the Atlantic Cable, such will make a show, and do to talk about; but, when thoroughly tried, the system will not be found to work well.

Now for my friend, Col. Chas. McLemore. The Chambers Tribune speaks nothing but the truth, when it says, "he was no ordinary man;" and if Chambers has not been left an orphan, the orphan's friend has left Chambers. I knew him when he was a little boy; his father died when he [Charles] was very young, leaving him and another,

Frank, to make their way through the world as best they could.

Charles McLemore was most emphatically what the world terms a self-made man.   He was endowed by nature with a fine intellect, and with that great share of moral honesty which has marked all of his family whom I have known, (and I have known many of them.)   He raised himself to what you have seen and know of him.   I am unable to say anything that could raise Charley McLemore any higher in the estimation of those who knew him, than the position he occupied at his death.   When I left Georgia, and made Alabama my home, Charley was a little boy; I think he then lived in Jones county.   Some twelve years afterwards, I met an intelligent young man at an Indian Council at Oweatumka-chee, or Falls of Little Uchee Creek, (where my old friend and camp-mate, Col. Henry Moffett, afterwards erected some mills.)   This young man was Charles McLemore.   I there renewed my acquaintance with him.   What I am now going to relate will be remembered by many now living.   The Council was in the fall of 1832.   Some Cherokees had been invited or requested by the whites to attend the Council, in order to encourage the Creeks to emigrate.   Among the Cherokees were old Ridge, and his son, John Ridge, (who has been killed since by the Ross family in Arkansas,) Davy Van, and others.   The Creeks were soured, and I knew it—for I lived within two miles of the head chief, and knew his feelings, and communicated them to Col. Crowell. He soon discovered the great disinclination the chiefs had to going into Council, and used every exertion to prevent liquor being brought into camp.   But by some means, some negroes belonging to a half breed, Joe Marshall, got some whisky into camp.   There was an order for it to be destroyed, and the whisky was poured out on the ground, which seemed not to suit the tastes of some whites as well as Indians.   It appeared that a white man had hired the negroes to carry the whisky to camp, and it was proposed to flog the negroes; but Marshall objected, stating that the white men were to blame. A general fight commenced with the Indans themselves and a great many whites left the camp, not knowing but that a general massacre was to take place. Marshall's party was the weakest, and seemed to be giving way. I remarked to McLemore, who was standing by me, that Marshall was a good man, and had been a great friend to the whites in the Creek war, and that I disliked to see him backed out; that was enough—Charley walked into the thickest of it, among knives, clubs, and everything else. Wherever he went, he opened their ranks, and Marshall soon quit winner. That was Charles McLemore. I have seen some trouble, and think I know something of men; but there is not one in a hundred who would have risked so much and showed the daring that McLemore did that night, and under such circumstances. Peace to the good and brave.

Yours, &c.,

T. S. W.

APPENDIX.

It is thought best to give, in this Appendix, the letter of the late Col. Pickett, to which Gen. Woodward makes frequent allusion in the foregoing pages. As a matter of local interest, too, a valuable letter from Mr. Klinck, of Tennessee, is inserted ; and there are added several letters lately received from Gen. Woodward, himself.

J. J. H.

COL. PICKETT TO GEN. WOODWARD.

MONTGOMERY, February 23, 1858.

Dear Sir :—About one month since, I placed in the hands of our mutual friend, Mr. Hanrick, a copy of the History of this State, with the request that he would mail it to you, in conseqvence of the very long acquaintance which has existed between us. I hope that you have received it, as you state that you have never read it. If you will peruse it connectedly through, as it is a connected work, you will arrive at the conclusion that you and I differ very little, or if at all, only on some unimportant points. In your letters, recently published in the Montgomery Mail, which have interested many of the old settlers here, (and which we hope will not be your last,) you took issue with me in regard to some things connected with the Creek and Alabama Indians, while you agree with me in others. In regard to the manners, customs and traditions of these tribes, you and I are as well acquainted as any two men of modern times, and I think if you understood what I have published of them, not the slightest difference would exist between us. If you had read the work I have sent to you, your memory, always most excellent, would have been so refreshed that the connected narrative of the work, well supported by every authority which patience, time, labor, and the use of money could procure, would have brought you to the conclusion that we agree on all the important subjects there narrated.

One of my main authorities for what I have written on the Creek Indians, and the smaller tribes who lived in their confederacy, was the old agent, Benjamin Hawkins, whom you acknowledge to have been the wisest and most reliable man you ever knew. I was furnished with his "Sketch of the Creek Country" in his own hand-writing, which he gave to his cotemporary and illustrious friend, Andrew Pickens, of Revolutionary memory. In addition to this rare and valuable document, I procured from Paris a history of the Creek Indians, written

and published by Gen. LeClerc Milfort. He had lived in the Creek
Nation from the period of 1776 to the period of 1796. He married
the sister of Gen. McGillivray, who was a mixed blood Chief of great
talent and renown, of whom you have heard, but who died some time
before the period of your birth. No two authorities could be better
than these. Hawkins had been appointed Creek Indian Agent in Washington's administration, and had grown grey in their service until the
times in which you made his acquaintance. Milfort had lived in the
Creek Nation for twenty years; he was a scholar and a fine writer, and
had fortified eimself with the most remote traditions, and with all the
knowledge which Alexander McGillivray himself had collected in regard to the history of his formidable tribe.

In your published letters, you have also alluded to the invasion of
Alabama by Hernandez DeSoto, and to what you *suppose* I have written
on that subject, judging from my letter to Mr. Hobbs, of the late House
of Representatives. You state that you have never read a complete
narrative of that expedition. In the account I have given in the History of this State, I am sustained in every particular, by the best authorities an author ever had, or could desire. I mean by the authority
of *eye-witnesses*. Among the expedition of DeSoto were FIVE men,
learned and reliable, each of whom kept a daily journal of the directions which the army took, the rivers it crossed, with their names; the
towns through which it passed, with their names; and of the various
tribes through whose territory it passed; and of the battles which it
fought with them. Three of these Spanish cavaliers, on their return
to Spain, placed their several accounts in the hands of Garcellasso de
la Vega, an eminent writer, who published a history of the expedition
in Spanish. That history is now in my library, in the French language.
Even the Commissary of DeSoto's expedition—Louis Hernandez de
Biedma—furnished an account, which is now in my library. Then I
have in my library, the journal of the remaining fifth man, a gentleman
of Elvas, in Portugal, who seems to have accompanied the expedition
more as a journalist than as a warrior, and whose statements seem to
be very accurate and minute.

In your published letters in the Montgomery Mail, you also refer to
me in connection with the manuscript of the late George Stiggins, and
state that you understood I borrowed it when I wrote my history; and
in one of your private letters to Mr. Hanrick, you ask what has become of it, and whether Stiggins is yet alive? You remember that
when the French colony of Louisiana, about Natchez, had been destroyed by the Natchez Indians, and in return had been nearly destroyed by the French, that those who remained alive fled to the Chik-
asaw nation for protection, and as a place of asylum. Some of that
Natchez tribe fled to a portion of the Creek Confederacy, in what is
now Talladega county. They there erected a town, and called it Nau-

che, and it was there that George Stiggins was born—his father being
a Scotchman, and his mother a Natchez Indian. When Stiggins at-
tained to manhood, he was living on Little River which separates Monroe from Baldwin county, in Alabama. You know that a great many
of the wealthy half bloods lived there. When the General Government, a long time afterwards, made a treaty with the Creek Indians, by
which the Government agreed to allot them sections and half sections,
you remember that Mrs. McCombs, Durant, Stiggins, and others, removed to East Alabama, to become possessed of their allotments under the treaty. Stiggins was then writing his History of the Creek
Indians. Some time after you removed from Alabama, he died, and
left his manuscript in an unfinished state. I endeavored to get possession of it, to aid me in the work I have published, but the family,
attaching great importance to it as a *valuable* relic, I never could use
it, and never did use it. I was, however, one day at the house of Stiggins' son, and he let me examine it for an hour. I found that I had
already obtained all the valuable information which Stiggins disclosed,
through Hawkins' "Sketch of the Creek Country." The manuscript of
George Stiggins consists, if I recollect correctly, of eighty-one pages
of closely written foolscap paper—hand-writing good, but prepared
in such a style as an old-field school master would use. The facts are
no doubt valuable, and being written by an Indian—a native of Alabama—the Historical Society of this State ought to purchase it, and
publish it as it is written. It is in the possession of some of that family now living on Little River.

Truly your friend,
ALBERT J. PICKETT.

P. S.—If you furnish any more communications to the Montgomery
Mail, (and I hope you will,) please give all the information you possess
in reference to that singular tribe, the Uchees, who once lived in the
territory of the present Russell county. That tribe has puzzled me
more than any other tribe which has ever lived on Alabama soil. And
tell us (if you know) why it was that nature gave them the poorest
and most discordant language which any tribe ever before, or since,
has employed. A. J. P.

From the Montgomery Mail, February 27, 1858.
GEN. TOM WOODWARD'S INDIAN HISTORY.

Eds. Mail:—I have been much interested in the letters from General
Tom Woodward, which have appeared recently in your paper; and I
am induced to offer you the following items, hoping thereby to elicit
something more on the same subject:

About one year since, I passed a night at the house of Mr. Stephen
Richards, in West Florida, who was an interpreter during the Semi-

nole war, and had passed much of his life among the Indians. He gives the same account, substantially, of the migration of the Indians from west of the Mississippi, that Gen. Woodward does.

I think he locates the Yemasses—I write from memory—in the Middle and Eastern portions of Flórida, and says they were occupying the country when the Creeks came. He describes the Yemasses as having dark skins, coarse hair, thick lips, and *flat* feet, and as having inferior implements of war to the Creeks.

A war of extermination was waged by the Creeks against the Yemasses, and finally, at Tallahassee, the last of the warriors were killed —but about a thousand of the young Creek warriors took sweet-hearts among the Yemassee girls, and saved them from death. According to a law among the Creeks, these were required to remain out of the nation a year for purification. Before the end of the year, the young warriors concluded to make wives of the Yemassee girls and set up as a nation for themselves, which they did. The Creeks called these warriors *Seminoles*—meaning *wild*, wild man, crazy, mad-man, &c., &c. These Semlnoles were afterwvrds joined by the outlaws and runaways from all other nations, and soon became a formidable nation, as Uncle Sam knows.

Col. Woodward speaks of the Seminoles as a mixed race, and gives the meaning of the name as wild, or runaway, or outlaw. I presume this is the race we know as the Seminole.

Those best acquainted with Indian history and customs, &c,, of this region, are rapidly passing away, and it would be interesting if they could meet, compare notes, and give us a correct account.

J. W. K.

From the Montgomery Mail, Nov. 24, 1858.

LETTER FROM J. G. KLINCK, OF TENNESSEE.

Eds. Mail:—Having lately read some sketches of the Creek Indians, in the early history of Alabama, from the pen of the well remembered Gen. Tom Woodward, I have dared to presume that a few facts in relation to the first settlement of your town will not prove uninteresting to some of your readers. At the time of the great influx of emigration from the States, in the early part of 1817, I left the old South State, with the intention of proceeding to Fort Claiborne; but after a tedious journey of twenty-two days, I crossed Line Creek and made a halt at the fork of the road leading to Fort Jackson, and occupied a tenement belonging to Mr. Evans, who was then keeping public house. One hundred yards from this spot, and on the Federal road leading to Claiborne, was the firm of Meigs & Mitchell, and one mile on this road, East, on Milly's Creek, was James Powers, who did a large business in groceries and provisions; further East was Major Flanagan, (small trader,) then came Arterberry, and Denton, or Dent, who occupied the land and owned the ferry on Line Creek. With myself, the above were the only traders nearer than Fort Jackson. While here, and immediately after the first land sales in Milledgeville, the same summer, Mr. Andrew Dexter, of Massachusetts, and a Mr. Spears, of Oglethorpe county, Ga., came to Mr. Evans', both being attacked with bilious fever, (Dexter slightly,)—they were en route to view their purchases at the time. Mr. Spears occupied a bed in the same room in which I had my goods, and never left it until his death, which was about two weeks after his arrival. He was prescribed for by an eminent physician (Dr. Dabuy) from Virginia, and had every attention paid him by Mr. Dexter and the family of Mr. Evans.

After this occurrence, Dexter proceeded to examine his purchase, and soon returned, being much flattered with the prospect of its advantages for a town site, and its central position for the Court House, when the county became sub-divided. He communicated all his plans to me—that we were jointly to use our influence in drawing all the traders to the place intended for the town, which would necessarily draw the trade to that point, except from those on the road near Line Creek. I advised him to visit J. C. Farley, Carpenter & Harris, Laprade, (traders) and Dr. Morrow, a practising physician, offer each a lot gratuitous, and proceed immediately to lay off the town.

My then locality was an unenviable one, so I immediately removed my goods to James Vickers', who lived on the bluff above the intended town. Dexter soon obtained the services of a Mr. Hall, surveyor, who laid off the town. As soon after this as I could have the center pointed out to me, I selected my lot, which was a privilege of first choice, and to name the place, which I called New Philadelphia—and the name was never changed until 1819. I employed a Mr. Bell to build me a cabin—and in showing him where, we found on the corner a post or black oak in the way of laying the ground sill, when I immediately seized the axe and felled it, remarking to Bell, "this is the first tree—future ages will tell the tale." The house was built, and a well dug close by, at the junction of Market and Pearl streets. Dexter, before I could occupy the house, wishing to place it upon a more elevated portion of the quarter section, employed Mr. John Blackwell to re-survey it, which he did, and I took my first choice again, built another cabin and occupied it. After I built the first, and a little before I had occupied the last, J. C. Farley had a frame store house put up, which was weather-boarded with clap-boards, but never occupied until after I had completed and was doing business in my second tenement.

Next came Carpenter & Harris, John Falconer, John Goldthwaite, Eades, Dr. Gullett, James Vickers, 'Squire Loftin, John Hewett, Teague —the first five were merchandizing. During this time the Scott & Bibb Company, as it was called, from Milledgeville, in Georgia, had bought largely of lands, and among others the fraction that was situated on the bluff, between Dexter's quarter section and the river, for which they were to pay, as I understood, $50 per acre—if so, it accounts for their having tried to build a town below then New Philadelphia, called Alabama, to rival the former or possibly impede its growth ; but it was no go, as all the traders were in New Philadelphia, with the solitary exception of a man by the name of Campbell, with a few goods, among a few private families ; they being his only customers, he soon abdicated, either for want of goods or patronage.

The business of locating a site for a Court House came, and commissioners were appointed for that purpose. Public opinion had given the Court House to New Philadelphia, whose citizens, generally wide awake to their interest, by way of inducement, entered into a bond of $20,000, payable to the Commissioners for the purpose of building a Court House and Jail, if they would locate the buildings in the last mentioned town, on the hill, where a public square had been laid off for the purpose. This bond was signed by Dexter, J. C. Farley, John Falconer, Harris & Carpenter, and myself, taking a mortgage of the lots around the square as an indemnity in case the proposition had been acceded to by the Commissioners.

From some cause or other, (I will not say prejudice or interest.) "Yankee Town," as it was sometimes called, did not get the Court House, with all its offerings, but it was awarded to Alabama Town. Up to the fall of 1819, no Court House had been built; a log building resembling an ordinary corn-crib, was used as a Jail ; Justice's Court was held in Judge Bibb's house, and the first Circuit Court was holden in Mrs. Moulton's house, by Judge Martin, if the name be correct.

The residents of Alabama Town, as far as I can now recollect, (in the fall of 1819,) were Capt. John Goss, (Gause ?) and family, William Goss, James Goss and family, old lady Goss and her daughter, Eliza, (who that fall married Willburn,) Major Peacock and family, Mr. Ashley and family, Mr. Jones and family, a Mr. Perry, Judge Bibb, Major Johnson, (Mail Contractor,) Edmondson, Clerk of the Court, and his mother-in-law, Mrs. Moulton—an entire military and civic population— no merchant or trader in town.

Such as I can now name of the inhabitants in Montgomery, (now called,) are Dexter, Loftin, first Justice in town ; James Vickers, innkeeper ; Thomas and William Lewis, merchants ; Major Wood, planter ; Stone, (son of Judge Stone, and son-in-law of Esquire Loftin ;) Eades, merchant ; Drs. Gullett & Co.; J. C. Farley, merchant ; Carpenter, merchant ; John Falconer, merchant, and first postmaster ; Dr. Morrow ; J. Goldthwaite, merchant ; John Hewett ; Widow Hewett and family ; Mr. Larkin, inn-keeper and farmer ; Henry Farley, brother of J. C. Farley ; A. M. Reynolds and family ; Mr. Baker ; John Belew, carpenter ; R. Mosely, and a number of other families of same name, on the Hill ; Nimrod Benson, Esq. ; Esquire Sims, attorney ; and a dense population—I cannot recollect names.

It will be well to mention how the town happened to change its name. As early as January, 1819, Dexter came to me after I had held a conversation with one of my other friends on the subject, and told me a proposition had been made by the interested of Alabama Town, (the Scott Company,) to annex the Bluff fraction to Dexter's quarter section, which they had forfeited and since entered, and were willing to locate the Court House on the line of fraction and section, each holding their own territory. Well, believing it not a very hard matter to move a Court House which had never been built, but a right which that company had to pick it up and set it down wherever they pleased, I concluded it might be more to our advantage to have one in which they were interested, than one entirely our own. All was agreed, and the union took place. Now for the name : What shall be done ? It will never do to call it "New Philadelphia," nor "Yankee Town ;" either scent too strong for "Georgy." I have it—we will call it Montgomery, after the county ; it was settled upon without a dissenting voice, and to the great satisfaction of all concerned—the name being equally dear to every American throughout the land. Thus, by the unity of interests and joint fellowship, has this town continued to grow ever since, in wealth and population.

I could speak, if I had time, of the many pleasing associations of that day and place ; but must conclude, by insisting that the palm of its early time and prosperity belongs to Andrew Dexter and his then associates.

P. S.—The foregoing alludes to Dexter's quarter section alone, up to the time stated. Walton Lucas and Mr. Allen were both doing business on the Bluff fraction, in 1819, close to the river.

LETTER FROM GEN. WOODWARD.

WHEELING, WINN PARISH, LA., }
December 8, 1858. }

J. J. HOOPER, ESQ. :

Dear Sir:—I some time back wrote you a letter, in which I mentioned that I was glad to learn that my friend Hanrick was still living, and that he had informed me he was the only one living in Montgomery who was at the place when he came to it, which I think was in 1817. I also stated that Arthur Moore was the first white man who built a house and lived in it, at the place the city of Montgomery now occupies. I still assert it; for I distinctly recollect stopping with Moore, and killing two deer, in a small pond that stood a little North

9

of where Mrs. Reed kept a tavern* when I left the country.   Mr. Hanrick can point out the spot where the pond was.

In that letter, I had no idea of differing from Mr. Klinck as to how
New Philadelphia (as it was then called) was laid off, or by whom.   I
wrote you long since that Andrew Dexter was looked upon as being
the true founder of Montgomery.   My first visit to the spot where
Montgomery now stands, was in April, 1814 ; it was then called Chun-
nanugga-Chatty, or the High Red Bluff.   From that time until I left
Alabama, I was as familiar with the place as I was with very many of
its inhabitants.   It only seems to be a test of memory, or recollection,
with those who write about the early settlement of Montgomery.   Keep
out Col. Gilbert S. Russell, of the old 3d regiment of U. S. Infantry,
and I will risk my own memory against all others, for a correct narrative of what I knew in early life, whether it be interesting or not to
those who are living.

Mr. Klinck mentions many names that are as familiar to me as my
own.   In case this should ever be published, I will give a few partien-
lars which will be remembered by those who lived some thirty-five or
forty years back, and longer, if you choose.

I recollect Col. John Blackwell, whom Mr. Klinck speaks of.   I beat
him running a foot race at Old Alabama Town, on the day that James
Johnson and Henry D. Stone ran for the office of Colonel.   I recollect
that a Mr. Clay killed Dr. Sidneyham about the same time.   The Dr.
was a brother-in-law of Col. John Blackwell.   I recollect Adams and
Madison, whom he mentions ; they were both about as ugly as mortals
ever get to be.   I knew the Irishman, John Conden ; and bought his
dun pony, which will be remembered as well as Conden himself.   I also
knew all of the Evans', Tatums, Fitzpatricks, Gosses, and Laprade.   I
knew him while he was a Commissary in the army, long before Montgomery was settled by the whites.   Jesse Evans was considered the
best fist-fighter of his size, in his day.   Organ Tatum and Ben Ward
had the first fist-fight I ever heard of, in Montgomery county.   Tatum
bit off a piece of Ward's nose.

I also knew Bob Moseley.   Some one stole a fine hound from me in
Milledgeville, Ga., which I purchased from a man on Lyrick's Creek,
S. C., some years before that.   I found the dog in the possession of
Mosely, in Montgomery, and we were very near having a serious diffi-
culty about it.   I proved by Col. Freeny that the dog was mine.

It was Joe Fitzpatrick who was the competitor of Major Pinkston,
and not Phil. ; nor was Phillips Fitzpatrick the father of Senator Ben,
but both he and Joe were the older brothers of the Senator ; and all
were the sons of William Fitzpatrick, a good old Washington and Adams Federalist ; and both Joe and Phil.—who had much to do, at an
early period, in the shaping of Alabama politics—were John Quincy

---

*Opposite the "Montgomery Hall."

Adams men, in opposition to Wm. H. Crawford, the regular Republican nominee for President. to succeed Mr. Monroe. But both were Jackson men after that.

I could give you a long string of Jeffersonian Democrats, both in Alabama and Georgia, who have descended from old Adams Federalists; but it is of no use now, as the National Democracy, South, is fixing to take up Mr. Douglas, who has done so much for the South; for under his especial management, a few Southerners at least have been permitted to live out a short and precarious life in Kansas, with a few slaves. That, and the whipping of old Greely and Sumner, are achievments of which the South can boast; and if Mr. Douglas is the next President, the South may be able to crow over many other such victories.

As to the few sketches I have given you above, about the early set-tlers of Montgomery, if you can find any one who can go further into little particulars than I can, I am willing to quit; for I am certain that such is not very interesting.

My health is improving, and I hope that I shall yet see Montgomery once more, before I take my departure for that better city which we read of.

I am now fixing for hunting. I have fourteen fine hounds, a good horse and gun; and, as for fishing, there is a place near me that even Peter of old would not risk his net in, if he knew how plenty they are. But notwithstanding all the fine hunting and fishing, as well as the balance of the good things, Alabama and Georgia are preferable places to Louisiana and Texas, at least for me to live in. My advice to such as have advertised their lands for sale from choice, in Alabama and Georgia, is to withdraw their advertisements, pay up the printer, and content themselves where they are.

Your friend,   T. S. WOODWARD.

———

Wheeling, Winn Parish, La.,
December 13, 1858.

J. J. Hooper, Esq.:

Dear Sir:—Your letter of the 27th of November last came to this office some days back, and I would have tried to answer it before this, but have been too feeble to do so; and I now fear that I shall be unable to do justice to your inquiries, or answer them satisfactorily.

As to the correct date of my birth, there have ever been doubts, or differences of opinion among those who should have been best able to know the precise time I did come into existence. My father died, I think, on the 23d of March, 1800. I was then quite young, but recollect him very distinctly. Some two years after his death, my mother married a second husband. She lived but a few years afterwards, and then she died. I think she died in September, 1806. I was then left to work my way into eternity the best I could. So, you see I have got thus far through the journey of time, and from present appearances, it will not be long before I will have completed somewhat of a troublesome travel ; or at least I think many, to have performed the trip, would have taken much of the route to be pretty rough.

But iu order to account to you for the cause of there being doubts about the true date of my birth, I must here go into a few particulars of what I think was the cause. No doubt it will prove very uninteresting to you ; but in times past it was a matter of great importance to me and others. As this may be published, I go into these details for two reasons : The first is, it will do justice to the memory of one of the purest and best men that ever lived. The second is, that if I was dealt unjustly with when young, it will inform one individual at least, if no more, who is now living, that I was not so ignorant as not to know it.

My father was possessed, for the time and country in which he lived, of what was then termed a pretty little property. He made a will, the purport of which was about this : That his property should be kept together until his son Thomas arrived to the age of twenty-one years —(that was myself)—and then to be divided among the heirs equally. And in the event that I should die before I was twenty-one years old, the property should be kept together until the time I would have been twenty-one had I lived, and then to be equally divided among the surviving heirs.

At the time of my father's death the heirs were—my mother, a sister two years older than myself ; myself, and a brother three years, to a day, younger than myself ;—or at least I have been informed so by a Mrs. Black, whose authority I presume was better than any other, as she was present at the births both of myself and brother. Mrs. Black will be remembered as a very intelligent woman, by some in South Carolina, Georgia and Alabama. She was the mother of Major James Black, who was once, and may be yet, a citizen of Alabama. He resided either in Wilcox or Monroe county ; and a bluff known as Black's Bluff, took its name from James Black. I visited the old lady at her son's in Alabama many years after I was grown. She seemed to have a more distinct recollection of my brother's age than she had of mine, and said he was born in February, 1797.

Not long after my father died, my brother died also ; and my mother soon followed—leaving an only sister and myself. About this time, the settlement of Milledgeville, Ga., commenced. A sister of my mother, who was as good as God ever makes people, took my sister and raised her ; and I was left to "run in the range." But not long after my sister was taken to Milledgeville, a brother of my mother had me caught and taken there also ;—and if there was ever a better man than he, he lived before my time, or in some country which I have not been familiar with. He tried to tame me ; he sent me to school to one John Posey, who taught in the State House, then an unoccupied building. But I had been so neglected, and had grown to such a size—and finding boys greatly under my age and size so much further advanced than myself—it embarrassed me ; and every opportunity I could get to go into the country, and get with boys whom I could look upon as being more upon an equality with myself, I would do so. The older members of my uncle's family could see, notwithstanding the coarse and rough manner in which I had been brought up, that I had sense enough to know my true situation, and felt my inferiority.

My uncle, his wife, (whom I yet love as a mother,) and down to the youngest child who could talk, treated me with the utmost kindness, and tried to make me feel as their equal ; but I knew too well what I was, to be satisfied. I would play and frolick with his boys, to whom I became very much attached—in fact, I loved them like brothers— and to-day that branch of my mother's family feel nearer to me than any relations I have on earth—my niece, Mary Walker, excepted ; and she would not feel as near to me as she does, but for her present embarrassed situation.

This kind treatment of that family to me was kept up for some eighteen months or two years, when one of my uncle's daughters married Robert Rutherford. In him I found a true friend, such as orphans seldom meet with.

My uncle was now fixing to send his sons to Athens to school. I think a Dr. Brown was then at the head of that institution. Rutherford proposed to send me with the other boys, and my uncle readily agreed to the proposition. Preparations were making to send me to College—when another uncle, and a brother of the one I lived with, interfered ; he said it would be money thrown away, &c. I think this last mentioned uncle always had more control over the family than he was probably justly entitled to ; but so it was, and has been. I never saw the inside of a College but once, and that was but for a few minutes, as I only went in to help another boy carry out his trunk, which he was unable to carry himself.

My uncle who was so opposed to my being sent to school, employed me the next year to plow for him. I did him what I thought was a tolerably faithful year's work ; and at the end of the year, I proposed to have a settlement, or asked pay for what labor I had performed. But my uncle was by that, as he was by the school money—he thought it would be "throwing it away," and of course he never paid me one cent.

I then began to conclude that if I had to go through the world without any money being laid out on me, I had better try my hand with the Indians, as it was said they could get through life with less money than the white folks. From then until the Creek Indians migrated to Arkansas, I never lost an opportunity to make myself acquainted with their character and history.

In 1811 my uncle, with whom I had lived in Milledgeville, sent to my step-father—who then lived in Franklin county, Ga.,—and had four of the oldest negroes that belonged to the estate of my father carried to Baldwin county. He sold one of the negroes, purchased a tract of land, and put the other three negroes to work for the support of my sister and myself.

In 1812, the war with Great Britain commenced, and I entered the army as a private soldier on the 1st day of July of that year. I will here drop a few lines in relation to my old uncle, as well as a tear on this paper for him and Robert Rutherford; and the greatest favor that I have to ask of my creator is, to permit me to live until the first day of July, 1862, when I intend to visit the last resting place of those two men.

My uncle was a blacksmith in his younger days, and at the time I lived with him, he was getting to be an old man; and notwithstanding his age and very considerable wealth, he would frequently work in the blacksmith's shop—and it often happened that I would blow the bellows' and strike for him. I remember several times being with him in his shop, when he would stop work, wipe the sweat from his face, and look me sternly in the countenance, which would cause me to look at him. I could see the water rise in his eyes, and as soon as he discovered that I noticed it, he would step up to me, pat me on the head, and say, "never mind, my boy, you shall be a man some day." I at that time had no idea that the old man had any kindlier feelings for me than he had for any other straggling boy—but I was mistaken.

In 1813 my sister married Gen. James C. Watson—who, for the last fourteen years of his life, resided in Columbus, Ga. I at that time knew but little about my father's matters, more than that he had died possessed of some negroes and land; and Watson knew less than I did. The war was going on—I cared nothing about property—and if Watson wanted anything, or to know anything, of my father's estate, he was too proud to ask or make any inquiry about it. But I mentioned to Watson that I thought if right could take place, that my sister and myself ought to have something more than what our uncle had promised for us, and that I thought there was a will somewhere, and requested him to see my uncle on the subject; but he declined making any inquiry, and so the matter rested—and we went about dividing what little we had—that is, my sister and myself. Watson would not consent to settle with me, but insisted that I should have Robert Rutherford appointed as my guardian—I then weighing near a hundred and seventy pounds. Rutherford consented to act for me, and everything went on well; and the division was equally made. Rutherford then said to Watson, "take Tom's little matters into your hands, and pay what will be right; for he (alluding to me) will do nothing while the war lasts but follow the army."

So matters rested until 1815, when I was discharged from on board of that ill-fated vessel, Epervier, or El Epervier, (of which I will give you more in my next.) On my arrival in Milledgeville, I met with my old uncle; he seemed proud to see me, and said to me—"Tom, you are now a man; I want you to take your horse and go to Judge Screene's for a paper. If the paper is not in Screene's possession, do you give this to the Clerk at Saundersville,"—handing me a letter at the same time.

I went to Judge Screene's, and got the paper. It was my father's will, or a copy—I now do not recollect which—the purport of which I have given you before. I carried the paper to my uncle; he then said to me, "take the will, examine it, and get the advice of a lawyer, and do what you think best;" but said that he was certain that all the property of which my father died possessed, belonged to my sister and myself—as well as a portion of what my mother had, and was to receive from the estate of her father. And while I am at this part of my subject, let me say, for the information of some who are yet living, that neither myself or my sister ever received a particle of what belonged to my mother, except the milk we drew from her breast, and the few clothes she may have made for us when we were small children. Notwithstanding there was some valuable property which I was entitled to, I never asked for or tried to recover a cent of it. I know where it is. It is in the possession of a branch of my mother's family who are less entitled to it than any of the family whose hands it could have fallen into. I could yet recover it, were I so disposed; I know where the papers are, and could identify the negroes; but I was deprived of the use of it at a time when it might have been of some service to me; now I am old and fast becoming a fit subject for a wooden jacket and a hole in the ground, I would not fee a lawyer and break myself of one night's rest for as much money as Samson could have packed at the time he carried off the gate posts at Gaza.

This letter, or the greater portion of it, may be by some thought best let alone; but notwithstanding I have always been ready to oblige others, there are times when I feel greatly inclined to gratify my own feelings, and this is one of them. Should this ever be published, it will reach some for whom it is intended. I must confess that I am not one of that kind of christians who, when slapped on one cheek, turn the other, unless forced to do so.

I will now return to my old uncle and the will. The old man explained to me the whole matter—how he had acted, and from what motive. And he was a man who was never known to misrepresent things. I recollect his looks—I recollect his language—and I recollect my own feelings. His remarks to me were about these : "Tom, no doubt you do, and will think you have been neglected ; and you have to some extent a cause to think so. I and your uncle Ben Howard, (alluding to another brother of his,) are the only members of our family who ever liked your father, and were the only ones who did not oppose his marrying your mother. And it will do you no good now to know their objections, and therefore I will let that pass." I then said to the old man, that he need not keep it back, for I suspected that I already knew their objections to my father, and told him what they were. He then asked me how I had learned it. I told him that I had seen my father's mother, two of his own brothers, and a half brother, and had heard them speak of it ; and had also heard one of my father's brothers say as late as 1809, while passing through Milledgeville in company with Col. Obed Kirkland on their way to Mississippi territory, that if I would search when I got old enough, he thought I could find a will of my father ; and that he believed it was on record in Franklin county, Ga.   After listening to what I have just written, which I learned from the Woodward family, my old uncle Howard observed that I knew much more of my father's matters than he had any idea of, and that the objection alluded to on the part of the Howard family to my father, was in consequence of his blood. He admitted that my father was an intelligent man—well educated for the times in which he was raised, and that the family stood high in South Carolina—particularly in Fairfield District—and that the whole Woodward family, women and men, were whigs in the revolution.

I must confess that this pleased me a little ; but the idea of its being known or thought by my mother's family that I was of a mixed race, annoyed me much. It was a thing that I had learned among the first things I did learn of my father's family ; and in my raising I avoided ever letting it be known to any but my sister, who knew as much about it as I did.

My uncle Howard said to me that my father had left him his Executor, but that he lived at too great a distance to attend to the matter, and that my mother had married a second time, and there were younger children of hers, and they were left motherless at an early day ; that he had concluded to arrange it so that when I became of age, the will should be placed in my possession, and let me take my own course. And that he would have been willing and was anxious to have educated me at his own expense, had I shown any disposition to study or fondness for books ; but that I had shown such a disinclination to go to school, and a disposition to ramble on the frontiers and loiter about the soldiers' and Indian camps, that he concluded to let me go, as it would have required measures more harsh than he was willing to use to restrict me ; and said to me if I had, from the neglect of friends and my own imprudence, been deprived of the use or knowledge of books

I had been to a school where no doubt I had learned much of men, and that he hoped in the end would answer me as well as if I had been sent to College. That good old man was right, and God has blessed him long since.

My uncle said I was then of age—Gen. Watson took the will and demanded the property of my father from my step-father ; a record of my age was produced, showing that I was born on the 22d of February, 1797, and my step-father claimed the right at least to keep the property together until February, 1818, Watson said—for the property and that suit were never determined.

In 1817 my step-father died. I was then a Major, commanding a detachment of militia in the U. S. service. In February, 1818, I borrowed a few days from the service, and went to Franklin county, Ga. The negroes had been scattered—some in Franklin, some in Elbert, some in Pendleton District, S. C., and one of them in the neighborhood of Tuscaloosa, Alabama. I had heard it said that there was one thing which had helped to make Gen. Jackson a great man—and that was the incurring of responsibility. So, whenever I found a negro, I laid hold of him, and succeeded in getting all but two. The one which was in Tuscaloosa was sent to Milledgeville by the man who held him in possession, on my giving him to understand that he or I would be put to some trouble, if the negro was not forthcoming, and that in a short time. The negro was soon in the possession of Gen. Watson, where I had placed the others. There was then one missing—a man by the name of Jim, whom we never got. The last I ever heard of him, Jim was given to Felix Grundy, by Swan Hardin, as a fee in a case where he [Hardin] was tried as accessory, before and after the murder of the Porters' by his [Hardin's] sons ;—that was in Columbia, Maury county, Tennessee, many years ago.

The negroes were placed in possession of Gen. Watson, as I before remarked ; we claimed nothing for a tract of land as valuable as any in the country at that time ; we asked nothing for the hire of some valuable negroes for near twenty years. But still there was a hatred entertained towards me by some who never had cause to owe me ill-will. Watson was getting up in the world a little too fast—becoming a little too popular, though a Federalist and a Clark man ; and in fact, I have often thought that that party in its purity was as good, if not better than the opposition—though I was not brought up in early life to think so. You have no doubt read of Judas, the traitor who betrayed his master, for a trifling sum of money. I have often thought that some more favorable allowances should have been made for Judas by the christian world, when we take into consideration with whom he was raised, and how he was brought up in early life. If the whole twelve had been Judas's who traveled with that good man—for a good man he evidently was—and whose great object was to reform the degraded habits of his countrymen, and to relieve them from their then embarrassed condition, and place them upon an equality with the other more enlightened nations of that day, and in which cause he lost his life. I have known some men, and had to do with them, who would have betrayed that good man in less time, and for less than half the amount that poor, ignorant Jew received.

We were sued, or attempted to be sued—much harrassed, and run to much expense; but we held the property. By the time the matter was ended, I had gambled and frolicked off my portion of it; or at least, the amount of it. I sold my interest to Watson; he paid me more than it was worth, besides doing me many other favors.

Now, sir, why I have written this long letter, which will be found of little interest, is, that Watson and myself have been often accused of having swindled a half brother and sister of mine out of property which was justly theirs; and it has also been said that after he and I had swindled those children, that he had swindled me. There is not a word of truth in the whole of it; and those who have made these charges against either of us, have ignorantly erred or wilfully lied.

Gen. Watson was the person I alluded to in the first part of this letter, and whose memory I wished to do justice to. He died in 1843, and was possessed of a handsome estate. It has been plundered, and partly by those who in his life time had received many favors from him. I know enough of those sycophantic, hypocritical scamps who used to crouch and receive favors at his hands, that have aided in reducing his only daughter to almost poverty; and they console themselves in their villainy by saying that he made his property by defrauding orphans. These men and a mismanaging husband could ruin the fortune of any child. All I have to say to such, is to keep a copy of this on hand, and when it comes to their turn to leave for a place which they will most assuredly dread, say to their children, should they have any to leave, that honesty is the best policy.

In my next, which will be in a day or two, I will give my age, or what I think it to be—a short sketch of my family on both sides—the wars which I have been engaged in—the fights that I witnessed, (which were but light)—what the S in my name stands for—my shipping on board the Epervier, and my discharge from her—my settlement in Alabama and Arkansas,--and all that you have requested to know; and I think you will find it much more interesting than this will be.

Yours, truly,

T. S. WOODWARD.

WHEELING, WINN PARISH, LA.,
December 20, 1858.

J. J HOOPER, ESQ.

Dear Sir:—A few days back I wrote you a letter, in which I promised, as early as possible, to give you a little sketch of my family, my age, and also the little wars that I was engaged in in my younger days. My name is not as common as Smith, but it is to be met with in all the States of this Union, as well as in many parts of Europe. Whether the name is Norman, Saxon, or German, originally, I do not know. But the name seems to have been derived from the occupation followed by those who bore it, at an early day. Woodward, one who protects the forest. My early ancestors of the name came from England, and settled in Maryland, under George Calverton, Baron of Baltimore. And near Annapolis, my great grandfather, Thomas Woodward, was born, and raised in Maryland. He raised a family of children by a first wife—she died, and he went into Fairfax county, Virginia, and married my great grandmother, Elizabeth Simpson, the descendant of a Scotch family—and Simpson is my middle name. Thomas Woodward and Elizabeth Simpson had one son, and called him Thomas, who was my grandfather. The old man returned to Maryland to move his other children to Virginia; he died on his visit to Maryland, and never returned, nor did his Maryland children ever get to Fairfax, but some years after their father's death, some of them went to Dinwiddy county, Virginia, and some to North Carolina; the North Carolina branch of the family has lost one letter in the name—they spell the name with one W, instead of two. I could name many of the older ones of most of the branches of the family, but it would take up too much time, as well as room, for a paper of this sort. My great grandmother remained a widow for some years, when she married a man by the name of Robinson, and raised two sons, William and John, both of whom I have seen, as well as their mother. My mother carried me and my sister to South Carolina when we were small children; the old lady was then living, and from what I have learned since, she was then about 112 years of age—she died two years after. It has been said that Robinson neglected my grandfather's education, and he was suffered to grow up very much in the way that one of his grand sons has since. At an early age he showed some inclination to become a soldier, and was in the French war, and a part of the time with Gen. Washington, who was then a Major or a Colonel. My grandfather was a Captain in that service, and was a much older man than Gen. Washington, and from what I have been able to learn from Parson Weems and others, the old man was looked upon as a good fighter. He married at an early age, a woman by the name of Jemima Collins, and they had four daughters and two sons, John and William. His wife died while he was in the service. At the close of the French war he was ordered on the frontier of South Carolina, leaving his children in Virginia. While in South Carolina, he became acquainted with my grandmother, who was his second wife. And it is the blood of that grandwother which courses through my veins, that in early life tempted me to quit what the world terms civilized and christian man.

I will now give you as accurately as I can the true history of that branch of my family. At the very earliest settlement of South Carolina by Europeans, and at the time those tribes of Indians that inhabited the lower parts of the Carolinas and Georgia, viz: the Sowanokas, Uchees, Yemacraws and others, a European, either of French or Spanish origin, by the name of Silves, (I think the name was originally spelled Silvester, but pronounced Silves,) came to Beaufort, S. C., took an Indian woman for a wife, and raised a family of children. About the time Silves's eldest daughter arrived to womanhood, an Englishman by the name of Thomas Stokes came to the country and turned Indian trader. Stokes took the daughter of Silves for a wife, and raised four children by her, two sons and two daughters, and one of them was my grandmother—her name was Elizabeth. She married one John May. The other daughter, whose name I have forgotten, (though I was much better acquainted with her than I was with my grandmother,) married a man by the name of Joiner.

The two sons were Thomas and Silvester. They were both Whigs in the American Revolution, and in a skirmish with some British and and Tories, at the old ridge, not far from the line of Edgefield and Lexington Districts, S. C., they were both badly wounded, and escaped at the time, but were necessarily forced, from their wounds, to go to a settlement to have them dressed. They were betrayed and taken prisoners by the British, and if not hanged at the same time with Col. Hayne, they were just before or after.

My grandmother raised three children by John May, two sons and a daughter, when May died. She then married my grandfather, and settled in Fairfield District—they raised three sons and three daugh. ters—my father was the oldest of the young set of children. My grandfather, after marrying my grandmother, moved his mother and two half brothers from Virginia to South Carolina. When the Revolution commenced, he raised among the first companies, if not the first, that was raised in South Carolina. He was killed on Dutchman's Creek, in a fight with the British and Tories, on the 12th of May, 1779. My half uncle, Ben. May, took command of his company. My half uncle, John Woodward, raised another company. My father, who was rather young at the commencement of the war to take the field, after his father was killed entered the service—his two own brothers being too young.

As many of the children and grand children of these men are now living, and know but little of the old stock, I will here give a list of the names of my father's family that served in the Revolution, and to a man I believe, were at the battle of Eutaw, except my grandfather and two grand uncles, Tom and Sil. Stokes, who were then dead.

My two half uncles, John and William Woodward ; my half uncle, Ben. May—(my half uncle, Tom May, was a cripple, and never served.) Now for the son-in-laws, or those that married my aunts. The oldest first: James Nelson, Phillip Raiford, Robert Rabb, James Andrews, Phillip Riley, William McMorris, William J. Augustin, Reeves Freeman, and Thomas Woodward, who was the youngest of the crowd, and my father. I have seen many of my grandfather's old company ; they were said to be good fighters. But I have heard the old ones say that my uncle Ben. May and uncle William Woodward were looked on as being the most daring men of that day.

My uncle William Woodward represented Fairfield District in Congress for several years, and the same District has been represented by his son Joseph, since, and it is his son William that represents Sumter county, in the Alabama Legislature. My mother was a Howard ; her father was Nehemiah Howard. a Virginian by birth, and of an English family. My grandmother Howard was Edith Smith, and descended from a Welch family ; it is said her father settled Smith. field, on Neuse River, in Johnson county, North Carolina. My grandmother Howard died in Milledgeville, Ga., very near one hundred years of age. I remember to have seen her mother when I was a small boy ; it was said she was over a hundred years old ; she was then a widow Edmonson. There were nine brothers of the Howard family, and five sisters ; they all lived to be grown and raise a family of children, except three—two uncles, one of whom was killed by a horse, and the other was drowned. My youngest aunt of that family was accidentally burned to death. My mother was the ninth child, and the first of the family that died a natural death. Maj. James Howard, late of Macon county, Alabama, was the next child to my mother, and was the last of the fourteen children to die, which was some two or three years back.

I think I have wrote enough to satisfy you that I have had, and yet have, some relations, though I seldom see any of them ; the balance I write now will be little things pertaining pretty much to myself.

Non long after the close of the Revolution, my father left Fairfield District, S, C., and went into Union District, and taught school ; several of the Howard family went to the school; among them was my mother, and the children younger than herself. The school continued for some ten years, and at the close of the school my father gave my grandfather Howard to understand that he wished to marry his daughter Mary. It was objected to by the whole Howard family, except John and Ben. Howard. My father returned to Fairfield, and my grandfather Howard moved to Georgia. My grandfather Woodward had a large property in land and negroes for the time in which he lived, and after his death and the close of the war, the heirs set about a division. There was soon a split between the white and Indian children. My father took a few negroes and left for the Cherokee nation. On his route he called at my grandfather Howard's who had then settled in what is now called Elbert county, Georgia, and within six miles of the head of Savannah River. My father tried a second time to get the consent of my grandfather, and through the influence of the two brothers, John and Ben, the matter was arranged. My father settled on Savannah River, between the mouths of two creeks, Lightwood Log and Powder Log, and in Elbert county. There had been at a very early day a stockade fort erected at the place by Gen. Perkins and Col. Cleveland—it was at the old Cherokee crossing, when that tribe was in the habit of trading to Ninety-Six, (96) or Cambridge, as it is now called. This old work stood near what was known in my time as Shockley's Ferry—the block-houses had been converted into dwelling houses—in fact, they had been put up first as dwelling houses and picketed in. In one of these houses I was born; an old lady by the name of Black was present—I have made mention of her before. I was born between the 22d of February, 1794, and the 22d of Feb., 1797, but it is impossible for me to know which, as there have been so many conflicting statements about it, for I rely nothing on any record that I have ever seen, and if I am to judge from what I can recollect of my father (who died in March, 1800) and other things, I am satisfied that I will be sixty-five years of age on the 22d February next. I do not claim to be born on that day, because the greatest man that our country ever had happened to be born on that day. All the old ones that I have talked to agree as to the day and month, but many of them differ as to the year. But there is one thing sure, I was born at some time and at some place, and if I don't find some time and place to die at, before a great while, it may be looked upon as a miracle.

I entered the army on the first of July, 1812, and accompanied Gen. Daniel Newnan to East Florida. I was in no fight in that expedition. I was at Kingsley's house, and in sight of Capt. Cone and his men when they had a little skirmish with the Indians, and Capt. Farren was killed. I went with some other militia under Tom Rix, to take a look at the castle of St. Augustine. We were taken for Cone's patriots, and were fired upon. If ever I see you, I will tell you an amusing story about that affair, but it would be too long here. I camped one night at Twelve Mile Swamp, with Sergeant McIntosh, and others, when the Indians or Spaniards fired a few guns at the camp, and made us leave. Some month or two after that, Dr. Fort, of Milledgeville, Georgia—who was a Captain at that time—and a Capt Williams, of the Marines, camped at the same place. They were attacked by a large party of Indians and Spaniards, and had a severe fight, and lost several men. Fort and Williams were both wounded ; Williams died of his wounds, and Fort, if living, will be a cripple for life. As to the fighting, I done but little and saw less; but if it was foot-racing, wrestling, swimming, and the like, I was among the foremost.

At the close of that expedition I returned to Milledgeville, half naked, half starved, and the ague and fever every other day. On my route home, I recollect to have met with Seaborn Jones, Bedney Franklin, (the Solicitor for that circut,) Peter Easly, (he was Judge,) a Mr. Sawyer, Hiram Stores, Tom Fitch, Stephen W. Harris, (the father of Wat. and Sampson)—all lawyers. I gave Jones the only trophy I had taken, in the war—it was a walking stick taken from the palm-tree—so you see I have borne off a palm in time of war, but never have been in a Legisleture or Congress like some, who have borne off perhaps less than a palm. My service was in 1813–14, under Gen. Floyd. I was in his night-fight, as it was called at Caleebe Creek—I know as much about that fight as any man living or dead. Barney Riley, a half breed, that killed John Lucas, and myself accompanied Captain Harvey one night from Fort Hall to Milly's Creek, just above the Federal Crossing, and took the wife of Ben. Moseley from the hostile Indians—killed three and crippled a few more. This trip to Milly's Creek was in February, 1814 ; the Caleebe fight was on the 27th Jan., 1814. The army returned home, and I remained, as I have before informed you, to take charge of Fort Hull.

After I returned from Fort Hawkins with Col. Milton's horse, as I mentioned to you before, I remained altogether with the Indians, until the last of April or first of May ; I then went to Georgia, remained a few weeks, and returned to the Nation, and spent most of the summer among the Indians. Some times I have been fired on by out-lying Indians—and some would have called them fights if they could have been got into the newspapers, before they got cold. That fall a call was made for troops to go to the City of Savannah. Capt. Horton, who commanded the Baldwin company, requested me to go with him as a kind of drill-master—not to go as a soldier in the service, but merely as a follower of the army—and that himself and officers would support me and give me soldier's pay themselves, as I would be entitled to none from the government. I declined the offer, but I met with a man by the name of Tom Cothron, who had just been in the State long enough to stand a draft, and it had fallen to his lot to take the field. He was somewhat afraid to risk his health in the winter season at Savannah, and wanted a substitute. He found a man that agreed to take his place for fifty dollars, but Capt. Horton would not take him. Tom Cothran was the stingiest man I ever knew, except Judge Smith and John Crayon. I promised Cothron to take his place for one hundred dollars, and he was to consider himself dead in the eye of the law should I be killed. The trade was made and in I went.

Militiamen, with a hundred dollars in their pockets, did not go in gangs in them days.

We reached Camp Covington—the Captain allowed me all the privileges that he dared to. I was soon detailed for a teamster, and it was not long before I was as well acquainted with Savannah and its inhabitants (the better classes excepted) as any one belonging to the army. I had a very fine suit of Indian 'fixins,' known to but few. There was a young man in Glasscock's company by the name of Augustus Parker, who had been raised among the Indians, and spoke the language much better than I could. There was a man in Horton's company by the name of Jacob Durden, a fine pensman, who wrote out a passport, and signed Col. Hawkins' name to it. With the aid of the Indian dress, Augustus Parker, and the forged passport, I imposed myself upon Gen. Floyd, and as many others as I chose to, and among them was Gen. Watson, my brother-in-law. I played it off upon the citizens of Savannah until I got tired. A great many of the tricks would have amused you, could you have witnessed them at the time. I was well acquainted with most of the officers and men that belonged to that army. It so happened that some of the officers of the army got to visiting a circus that was in the city, and had once or twice got into some little troubles with some naval officers, and a knock down or two had taken place, all being dressed in citizen clothes. A Major Mitchell, and some other officers proposed to take me along one night and pay my way to the circus, and if anything like a knock down took place, I was to lend a hand. I went, and after the show was over, all hands went to a drinking house, or grocery. We had not been there long before a dispute arose between the landsmen and seamen. The signal was given, and I let in on the little tarry-trousered fellows, and it was not long before I received a blow on the side of the head with a stick, which put me to some trouble to know whether it was the grocery or myself that was knocked down. But I soon found out that it was myself that had lost my balance, and called for quarter. Seamen are much more generous in a matter of that sort than landsmen, and they hauled off, and when I come to look around, my crowd had left. The seamen asked me who I was and what I was. I made a fair statement of the whole matter. They said I was a pretty good fellow, but could not be let off until I would go to a tavern and take something to eat and drink with them. I consented, thinking to get a chance to leave them. The tavern, I think, was kept by one Shellman.

Not long after we reached the tavern, a man by the name of Campbell came in. I knew him; he had been a soldier in 1812, under Col. John Williams, from East Tennessee. He informed me that he was then a marine, and belonged to the sloop-of-war Epervier, or El Epervier, and that much money was to be made by shipping on board of

her. I soon found that some of those who had been in the frolic at
the grocery were naval officers, for they would at times ask me if I
knew the penalty for striking an officer. They soon found that I
knew it was necessary for them to have worn some badge, so as to
distinguish them from other persons. So they resorted to the liquor,
and through that and Campbell, I suppose, I went on board. At all
events, the firing of the morning gun at Fort Wayne waked me. I
found myself roosting like a swallow, under deck, swung in a ham-
mock; I guessed what had happened. I went on deck, and felt, as
well as looked, pretty much like the fellow that took Aleck Mc-
Dougald's tumbler.

The news came that the British were about to force their way by
Tybee, and come to the city; they weighed anchor, took some soldiers
from Yellow Barracks and Fort Wayne, and put down the river. The
soldiers were put on shore at such places as they were needed. The Epervier was commanded by a Capt. Downs, who had been
with Commodore Porter at Valparaiso, and he [Downs] had after that
commanded the Essex, junior; the other officers on board that I became acquainted with were Lieuts. Shubrick and Stevens. The
Eperveir crowded sail and put to sea, as I thought. I seated myself
on a gun in the stern of the sloop—some called it the [stearn-chaser,
others the long Tom. But so it was, I sat on that gun and watched
the land until it looked about as narrow as a little blue stripe in a
home-made vest that I wore. It was not long before some fellow sung
out in the tops, "a sail in sight." The Epervier soon tacked and put
into Savannah. The sail that was seen was said to be a part of the
British squadron under the command of Admiral Cogburn, or Cockrain,
I forget which. I had been but a few days on board, and was ex-
tremly tired of a seaman's life.

By this time the news of peace had reached Savannah. I asked
permission of the Captain to go on shore and visit my friends at
Camp Covington, which he refused. The sloop was lying not more
than fifty yards from the shore, and I had not been on board long
enough to lose my action, or get the sailor's rock; and it so happened
that the Captain and Lieut. Shubrick went on shore in the yawl, and
the Captain's gig, as it was called, was lashed up to the sides of the
sloop. I watched my opportunity, took a running start, jumped upon
the Long Tom, and from that I jumped over the bulwark into the river, and swam ashore. Those on the sloop hollowed to those on shore
to stop me, but there happened to be a pile of staves close by, and I
gathered one and forced my way through their ranks. One fellow, to
be smart, followed me on horse back. I took him off, mounted the
horse and rode him a few squares, tied him to a post and went into a
hotel, kept by two ladies—Mary Williams and Becky Blackstrap.

10

They knew me, for it was at their house I had laid out the best part of Tom Cothron's hundred dollars. They dried my clothes, and that night I went to Camp Covington, and put up with one William Rice, a very good man—why I say he was a good man, I was with him several months in a militia camp, and he, like Elijah Moseley, would pray at night and fight in the day, if called upon—he was a good friend to me, at all events, and was for years after ; but when I rescued Henry Augustine, who was under guard for killing George Crookshank, I understood that Billy Rice became my enemy; but if he is living, and as good as I think he was, he no doubt has forgiven me long since. The last I heard of him he was a Methodist preacher, either in Autauga or Lowndes county.

I remained about Camp Covington until Gen. Watson could employ me a lawyer—he employed a Mr. Pelote. I then started for the sloop, which had dropped down to Five Fathom, near Fort Jackson ; I hailed her, and they asked what I wanted. I told them who I was, and they told me to come on board as I went on shore ; the weather was cold, but I took the water and reached the vessel. The Captain asked me why I had acted so. I told him I was drunk when I shipped, and that I had asked his permission to go on shore, and he had refused me the privilege, and that I wished to see my friends before I left—for it had already been understood that if peace was made with Great Britain, that the Epervier was to go up the Mediterranean with a fleet under Commodore Decatur. I was let off, and in a few hours two persons came along side—one of them was the Sheriff of Chatham county, John B. Norris. Norris was after that Sheriff of Dallas county, Alabama, and perhaps a merchant in Claiborne and Mobile. He served a writ of habeas corpus on the Captain ; I was taken to the city. I knew no one to give as security for my appearnce at court, and of course I was put in prison. I then would have been glad to be back on the ship. I was put in a room with three others—I shall recollect my room-mates as long as I live. There was one John Scales, and a man by the name of Phelps and Phillip Fitzpatrick. Scales and Phelps were charged with having sold be f to the British, while they lay off Sunberry, Fitzpatrick had killed a man by the name of McGraw, in Effingham county, and I for good behaviour

The jailor, or manager of the prison, was named McCall, and I think once wrote a history of Georgia. He was a bad cripple, unable to walk, and had to go over the floor in a little wagon constructed for the purpose, and a big negro man to carry him from one floor to another. Though, let me finish with my room-mates—Scales, Phelps and Fitzpatrick. They escaped from prison during my stay about the place. Scales I never heard of ; Phelps I heard was killed years after about Vicksburg, Miss.; and Fitzpatrick I think was the man that aided Gen. Jessup in procuring the Cuba blood hounds, in 1836. I had not been in my room but a few hours before I recognised the sentinel who guarded the door, or who was on that walk. His name was James Collins; I had known him long and well. I requested him to see Maj. McCall, and say to him that if it would not be deviating too much from his established rules, that I would be glad to be taken to where I could see him, if he could not come to the cell. In a few moments a Mr. Hanglighter, the turn key, and two soldiers, came and conveyed me to Maj. McCall. I made a fair statement of my case, and informed him that my brother-in-law was a Quarter Master at Camp Covington, and that if he would permit me to write, I could give any security that would be asked. I by chance mentioned that John Howard, of Milledgeville, was my uncle. The old man told me it made no difference about the security; if I wished to go to Camp Covington, there was his carriage horse, take him and go. I went, and it was late at night when I returned to the prison. I was then permitted to room with Mr. Hanglighter. I had some money, and lived much better than I had been in the habit of, for some time.

There were a great many British prisoners of war, as well as lots of Spaniards, Portugese, St. Domingo Negroes, and a few Turks, or some other copper-colored fellows from the Northern shores of Africa. Had it not been for the name of being put in jail, I was well pleased with my stay. I was permitted to visit my first room-mates whenever I wished. Every day such as were not put in for capital offences were turned out into the parade ground, as they called it. It was a strong picketing, enclosing two or three acres, and guarded by soldiers. I was allowed to go to the city whenever I chose, and stay as long as I pleased.

I got my Indian dress from Camp Covington, and Gus. Parker and myself performed one day for the Major. I had a large butcher knife, and the Major allowed me to act the drunken Indian. I got into the parade ground with my knife, and commenced cutting capers, and Parker telling how destructive I was when drunk. The British, Spanish, negro and everything else, would give me as wide a walk as I wished.

Now for the trial—it came off before Judge Berrien. While mixing about, I found a man who seemed to know my age better than I did myself, and all I had to prove was that I was not twenty-one years of age, to be discharged from the vessel on which I had shipped. The man that seemed to know my age was not a native of America, but looked old enough to have known Adam's age. He volunteered his services, and as the government had been receiving volunteers for some time past, I thought it well enough to take one into my service and drill him, and see what I could make of him. There was General Watson and a cousin of mine that could both say, from what they had understood, that my age was recorded some where as having been born on the 22d February, 1797—this was in March, 1815. I found that their testimony was not likely to do me any good. You know it has been said that volunteers are more reliable than drafted men. My volunteer came to the stand and made his statement. The Judge asked the witness some questions, as well as the counsel for Captain Downs. He answered them promptly, and to the purpose.

The Judge informed Capt. Downs that he should discharge me, unless he [Downs] could introduce testimony to set aside that of the witness who had just left the stand. Just as the Judge closed these remarks, the witness turned and said :

" Oh ! may it plase yer Honor, he may look all over old Ireland and Amaraky too, but he'll never find the lad that will say black is my eye."

Capt. Downs looked at the witness a moment, and then observed : " No, nor never can I, or any one else, find a man that is a better master of his trade than yourself."

The witness then remarked : " Ah ! captain, you are right ! There's not a man that lives can bate me a ditching, age and inch me."

These last remarks of the witness even made the Captain laugh. I was discharged. If I ever see you, and you will call my attention to this subject, and to the visit I made with Tom Rix to St. Augustine, and your risibility has not entirely left you, I will obligate myself at least to make you smile.

After I was discharged, I offered the Captain the money I had received as bounty money, but he would not take it, and insisted on my going with him, which I declined, and we parted. I have seen Capt. Downs since, but Lieuts. Shubrick, Stevens, and all that I knew on board, were lost. I believe I did hear that a young man by the name of Edward Collier, from Augusta, Ga., who shipped as Master of Marines about the time I left the ship, also left her before she sailed from Savannah.

On the 15th day of July, 1815, the Epervier passed Gibralatr on her return to this country with dispatches from Commodore Decatur, and was commanded by Lieut. John Shubrick ; that is the last satisfactory account that was ever heard of her; that is history. I have never let an opportunity escape to catch any thing that I thought would or could give the least clue to the destiny of that ill-fated vessel and crew.

After quitting the Epervier, and loitering about Savannah for a week or two, I returned to Milledgeville. I paid a visit to my relatives in South Carolina, and returned to Georgia and went into the Nation that same year ; laid a claim at or near the old Mordecai place, and very near where old John Burch settled. After spending some month or six weeks with the Indians, and engaging some corn, I returned to Georgia, and about the middle of December, 1815, I put out with two negroes for Alabama. On arriving at Line Creek, I learned from George Zimmerman or William Bagby that some one was on my claim. I concluded to locate among the Indians myself and send my negroes back, but had to carry them myself. I hired them to one James Mallett, for the year 1816; got two hundred dollars; put out next in company with Col. Turner Bynum and his son, Jesse A. Bynum, who since represented Halifax District, N. C., in Congress. I traveled with them to Tombecbee, or Bigby. The Indians stole our horses and hid them out, to get pay for bringing them in.

After Col. Bynum and his son left me I remained a week or two with an old North Carolina acquaintance, who was then living at Pine Jackson, a Dr. Neil Smith. From Pine Jackson I went to Madisonville, on Lake Ponchatrain, then to New Orleans. I there fell in with one Angus Gilchrist, and he and myself went to Nachadoches, Texas; there we found Edward McLauchlin, the best Indian interpreter I ever heard, except Billy Hamby. From Nachadoches we went everywhere. It would take one of John's kind of books to hold all that happened that year, so I will have to let that year's travel pass. Though it is not much trouble to say to you that I was long enough from home to get out of funds.

I returned to Georgia, and in November Gen. Clark and some other gentlemen employed me to go to St. Augustine after some negroes that had left them. I went to Camden county, and got a Captain Wm. Cone to go with me into Florida. I failed to get the negroes, but I saw Peter McQueen and Josiah Francis for the first time I had seen them for years, for it was before the war that I had seen them last. They were then trading at Fort Hawkins. They informed me that some of the negroes were on the Sawanee, at Bowlegs' Town. I returned to Milledgeville, remained a few days, went into the Creek Nation, and got a white man by the name of John Winslett, and we started for Sawanee. We got below Flint River, to Nehe Marthla's Town—or Fort Town—and found times a little too warm, and returned to Ochehaw, or Flint River. From there I went to Hartford, and Winslett to Chattahoochee.

Some time in January, 1817, I took a trip to North Carolina. I returned to Georgia in March, and was again prevailed upon to go to Florida for runaway negroes. I got a half-breed, named Laufauka—better known to the whites as John Blount—and an old Cusseta Indian named Tobler, who spoke fine English for an Indian—we put out and reached Bowlegs' Town. Arburthnot had a store close by, and he informed me that he believed the negroes, or a part of them, were in the neighborhood, but that I would hazard too much in attempting to arrest them. I quit the place, and saw nothing more of it for over a year, at which time I helped to burn up the place. I spent pretty much of that summer in the settlements on the Alabama river, and among the Indians. I made me another claim on the Autauga side.

On my return to Georgia, in the latter part of the summer, General Mitchell, who was then the Indian Agent, informed me that he had just received a letter from Arburthnot, stating that the Florida Indians would do mischief, and that he [Mitchell] had better caution the travelers on the Military Road, as well as inform our Government of their intentions. It was done, and a call made for troops. Baldwin, Hancock, Washington, Putnam and Morgan counties, had to elect a Major. I offered my services—my opponents were Capt. Joseph H. Howard, with whom I had served in two expeditions, and who was my Captain in both—and Capt. John D. Broadnax, a very efficient officer, who had distinguished himself in Gen. Floyd's fights. But it so turned out that I got more votes than both of them. Gov. Rabun declared that he was gratified at my success, and would issue a commission forthwith, that I should have the title, if nothing else.

The troops were not ordered out immediately, and I was made Deputy Sheriff of the county, bought an interest with one John Jeter in a tavern, had an interest in a Faro-Bank, and many other things to attend to, too tedious to mention. All these things, with the aid of my two partners in business, broke me, and I had nothing left but a Major's commission to depend upon. Finally, the troops were ordered to rendezvous at Fort Hawkins—I had nothing to do but leave a few debts unsettled, and put out. I happened to be the oldest Major, and there being no Colonel or Brigadier-General then at head-quarters, I took the command of two Battalions of Infantry, and two Troops of Cavalry. Shortly afterwards, a Mr. Wimberly was made Colonel, and Gen. Thomas Glasscock appointed to the command of the whole. The General and Colonel disagreed, and I associated mostly with a Capt. Melvin, who had command of a company of United States Artillery. There was little done except foot-racing, wrestling and drinking whisky, when we could get it. The troops never went more than forty miles beyond the line.

I will give you a few of the most remarkable occurrences that took place We traveled one day until after two o'clock, in a very heavy rain. The cavalry was some two miles in the rear ; the General ordered the men to fire off their guns, wipe out and re-load. I asked him if it would not be best to notify the dragoons, for fear they might think we were attacked, and make an unnecessary forced march to come up. The General said he commanded, and it was none of my business. The firing commenced ; some would re-load and fire ; after a little we heard a roaring behind us, and here was Major Lewis and Capt. Glenn—both uncles to Dixon H. Lewis—and very large men, and Glenn looked almost as large as the horse he was riding—and it was no pony, at that. They were both brave, and Glenn was a good fighter. I had seen him well tried at Caleebe Creek. Glenn did not care who commanded—he spoke his mind very plainly. The next firing we had we were encamped in a little breast-work—orders were issued for the sentinels to fire and run in, and a few in the line had private orders to fire their guns, in order to see how the men would stand it. It so happened that one of the sentinels did not receive the order, nor did he fire—his name was Booth Fitzpatrick, an uncle to Senator Ben. Fitzpatrick—and when the few in the lines commenced firing, all hands cut loose, and it was some time before a stop could be put to it. There were two cousins from Baldwin county, both very stout men and good soldiers—James Aldridge and Alexander Chambliss. Aldridge was a very mischievous youngster, and loved fun. Chambliss was very hard of hearing, and after the firing ceased, Chambliss asked Aldridge : " Jim, did you shoot?" " Yes," says Al- dridge, "I did ; and did you not see the Indians?" " No !" said Chambliss, "I did not shoot, nor did I see the first Indian."

After it was all over, Uncle Booth, as we all called him, came walk- ing in, and said : " My sons, I think you are mistaken, for I have look- ed with all the eyes I have, and have not seen the first Indian ; besides, my sons, you came very near shooting the old man, and if I had not placed a tree between you and me you would have done it."

The next thing worthy of notice, we left our ammunition at Black- shire's old breast-works, and marched some four or five miles and built a breast-work. The ammunition was guarded by some eight or ten men. One night we heard some guns in the direction of the ammunition camp, and it fell to my lot, or at least I volunteered, to go and see what the firing meant. I took these same two cousins, and some others, and put out. When I reached the guard, they had put up a target, and had been shooting at it by fire-light. So the General concluded that it would be easier to march back to the ammunition, than to remove it; so he did, and put up a little stockade-work, and called it Fort Early.

The next thing to be mentioned is, there was an Indian Town, some eight or ten miles below, on the river, and on the opposite side from us. It was called Fulemmy's, or Pinder-Town—the Indians were Chehaws. An officer and some fifteen men went down to get some provisions, and while they were there a party of hostile Indians, sure enough, made their appearance in the neighborhood of the town. The officer was notified of it, and fixed himself for a fight. They had expected to stay all night at the town when they went, but a runner was sent to camp for a reinforcement. It was then night, and thought not expedi- ent to march the men at that time ; I took with me an Indian boy or man, whom we had as an interpreter—one Abram Alfreend, and I think David Strother—and went down with the intention of moving the men out in the night. The runner and myself crossed over in a canoe, and found all safe, and when I got things ready for re-crossing, the canoe was missing. If the two big cousins were not in that crowd, I had them with me the next day. The old Chief told me there was a place just below on the river where I could wade across, if there was no canoe. The men said they could defend themselves, if they were attacked. I took an Indian with me, put on a blanket, and tied before me like an apron a woman's petty coat, and under the blanket I carri-

ed a musket, and the Indian carried a water jug. In making our way
to the ford, through some switch cane that a small foot-path went
through, at no great distance I heard a gun fire, and in my imagination
I heard others cock. That was enough for me. I dropped the blanket and petty coat, as well as the gun. I took the water—and whether
I waded, swam or forded, I never stopped to enquire, but crossed in
a hurry. It was but a little way to where I left Alfreend, the Indian'
and the other man ; we soon made our way to camp.

By the the time it was light enough to travel, and see what was
around us, we had a good force near the town. We crossed the men
over, found the trail of the hostile Indians, and pursued them until
late in the day—they going towards the white settlements, and rather
in the direction of our camp. We returned to camp that night, hun-
gry, wet and cold. Maj. Morgan had been out that day with a party
of men, and discovered their trail, and followed them until evening ;
he came in sight of their camp—they had encamped on a little ridge
of timber that was entirely surrounded by water, and within six miles
of our camp. The troops were anxious to go that night and surround
the camp, but it was objected to ; the next morning one of the friendly Indians whom I had left to follow the trail, came in and said they
had left, and had gone in the direction of Hartford. An officer and
some men were despatched to meet some provision wagons and let
them know that there was danger to be apprehended. The wagons
were met—a Maj. Franklin Heard had charge of the guard. They
reached Cedar Creek, within four miles or less of our camp, and two
men, Tom Lee and Sam Loftis, went into the creek, and had nearly
crossed, when they were fired upon and killed. They cut Lee's head
off, and scalped Loftis. The same man, Strother, whom I had with
me a night or two before, was along when the men were killed, and
brought the news to the camp.

Just before we learned that Lee and Loftis were killed, a man
named Keith had come through alone from Fort Gaines ; he had
travelled of nights, and wanted some assistance, as there were a great
many women and children unprotected in the Fort. I volunteered to
go, and my battalion was willing to go also, but was not allowed. I
then proposed that if the General would issue an order for me to take
the command at Fort Gaines, I would go alone, with the scout, Keith.
This he would not do, but said that if I could get thirty men, I might
have that number. I made a call, and got nineteen men—myself,
Keith, and Indian Bill, (the same man that saved Gen. Gaines' life
when his boat was wrecked,) making twenty-two.

As soon as they brought in Lee without his head, and Loftis scalped, we took a look and started that night. I crossed the river, went
to Chehaw, on Kitchafoony Creek, got fourteen Indian warriors, and
left next morning. I wanted, if possible, to cross before night, the
Echowagnotchy Creek, which was very large and very full, and a large

swamp on both sides. Between sunset and dark we entered the swamp. We had not gone far before we discovered some dozen pairs of Indian leggins, hung up to dry. We made our way to the run of the creek, and cut down a large hollow gum for the men to cross upon, but when it fell, it went so deep into the water that we could not use it, and we had to return back to high land and camp. Fortunately, we found a little wet-weather spring near the top of the most elevated point that we could find, and a number of dead pines that had fallen. We soon built a breast-work, and took our horses in, (there were but four)—and we concluded that if the worst came to the worst, as the saying is, we would try horse flesh. I slept very little that night. The old Chief whom I had along with me said he knew of a better and safer crossing place. Just before day we built up large fires, and left for the new crossing, which was about three miles. We crossed quite handy, and had to turn up the creek to get to our trail. A little after day we heard a number of guns fire in the direction of our camp—we made a forced march that day. We frequently, through the day, could see one or two Indians, who would keep at a distance from us. That night, about nine o'clock, we came in the neighborhood of Fort Gaines.

Now, sir, I have seen some trouble in my time, and have run some few risks, I reckon, and have often felt bad, but a portion of that night was the most disagreeable that I ever spent.

When we got within half a mile of the Fort, we could see dogs trotting, and hear them howling in every direction. Keith said the Fort had been taken. We got within three hundred yards of the Fort, and could see a dim light, that Keith said was in one of the block-houses. Keith approached a little nearer, and returned and he was sure the Fort was in possession of the enemy. I sent my interpreter and another Indian to the boat landing, to see if there were any crafts in which we could descend the river. They returned, and reported that there was a number of canoes and a ferry boat. I went a short distance to a spot that was a little lower than the surrounding earth, and wrote the following lines to Gen. Gaines, who was then at old Hartford, Ga.:

"JANUARY 16, 1818, 10 o'clock at night.—I am now within gun-shot of Fort Gaines, which is in the possession of the Indians. There is a heavy cloud rising, and as soon as it gets so dark that objects cannot be distinguished from the Fort, I will attempt to re-take it, and try and sustain myself until I get assistance. If I find I cannot do that, I will try and descend the river below Perryman Town, and go across to Fort Scott. I shall at all events sell myself and men as dearly as possible."

These lines I wrote by a little fire-light, kindled by the friendly Indians—they holding their blankets around it, to prevent its being seen from the Fort. I gave these lines to the interpreter, Bill—**gave** him my horse, and told him whenever he heard the firing commence, and was certain it was a fight, to make the best of his way to Hartford; but not to start until he was certain that the Fort might not still be in the possession of the whites, and by chance a sentinel or two might, through fear or something else, fire upon us.

The few lines above described as written to Gen. Gaines—and which you will see were not sent—are the only lines I ever attempted to write to a superior, detailing my situation. when on separate command, during all the service, or all the time I was in service. We waited until the cloud covered us, and then approached towards the the Fort, and when within about one hundred yards of it, I halted the men, and took Keith and an Indian, and made for a little flickering light which we could see, and which Keith supposed was in one of the block-houses. It turned out to be true. I walked up to the block-house, in which there was a door some three or four feet square, cut out to place a cannon at. Two men were playing cards on the ammunition box, and a young lady interesting them with a song. As I got to the door, one of the card-players observed to the other that he was out. I observed to them that it was me that was out, and wished to come in. I called up my men, took my letter to Gen. Gaines and burned it, and took command. I called up all hands, went to the magazine and took out some guns, and informed them that every man who did not take a gun and do duty, should leave the Fort.

I will here state that I believe I had as resolute a set of men for the number, as I ever saw. Among them was Capt. John Curry, from Washington; Lieut. Steel, from Hancock; Ensign Clark, from Morgan county, Georgia. I recollect yet many of the names. Catle J. Atkins, who lived many years in Macon county, Ala., and two brothers by the name of Emerson—Ben. and Uriah—who were living in Montgomery county, Ala., when I left the country, in 1841.

I remained at Fort Gaines but a few days, when I was relieved by Majs. Twiggs and Muhlenberg—Maj. Twiggs is now the distinguished Gen. Twiggs, of our Army. Maj. Muhlenberg is the officer who had charge of that convoy of boats, on one of which Lieut. Scott and his party were massacred. I marched my men to Fort Hawkins and discharged them.

I there met with three letters, one from Gen. Glasscock, requesting me to accept an appointment in his staff; one from Gen. Gaines, requesting me to get as many Indians as I could, and join him at Fort Early. The other was from Gen. Jackson—it was rather an order than a request. He wanted me at Fort Scott, with as many Indians as I could raise. I paid a short visit to Elbert and Franklin counties, Georgia, and to Pendleton District, South Carolina, after some negroes, of which I have before made mention. I passed through Twiggs county, Ga., got Capt. Isaac Brown and went to Fort Early. Flint River was very high, which enabled me to take a large flat boat down to Fort Scott, with ammunition for the troops. At Fort Scott I met with a portion of my Indians, which I had sent the talk to. I was placed at the head of the Indians, and crossed the river.

This was in March, 1818. We occasionally fired a few guns at straggling Indians, and they in turn would fire upon us; now and then one was killed, and a prisoner or two taken. There was nothing that could be called a fight on our route to the spot on the Apalacha-cola, where Gen. Clinch had blown up Fort Woodbine, a year or two before. The Army at that time consisted of the 4th and 7th Regiments of United States Infantry, two Regiments of Georgia Militia, under Gen. Glasscock, a Company of Kentuckians, under Capt. Robert Crittenden, and a Company of Tennesseeans, under Capt. Dunlap, (this last Company composed Gen. Jackson's Life Guard,) and some five hundred Indians, under the two half-breed Chiefs, Kinard and Lovet, and myself.

We set about building Fort Gadsden, on the site of old Fort Wood-bine. And at that place Gen. Jackson and myself took our first split, and as the matter has been often talked of, and misrepresented by some, I will here give you the particulars of that affair, as there are those yet living who witnessed it. Gen. Twiggs, of the Army, wit-nessed the whole of it, and Col. John Banks, of Columbus, Ga., Maj. Samuel Robinson, of Washington county, Ga., and Capt. Isaac Brown, of this State, are all familiar with the circumstances.

Capt. Dunlap was a gentleman and a good officer, and his company was composed mostly of the sons of the first families about Nashville, and some of them were very young, as well as very mischievous. They performed no duty more than to ride along the trail on our march, and when in camp strolled when and where they pleased. I had noticed them, or some of them, several times on our march from Fort Scott to where we then were, making fun and cutting their ca-pers with the Georgia Militia. I tried to put a stop to it as often as I could; told them that we were all engaged in the same service, and should be one people. It did no good. One day, while at work on Fort Gadsden, I had a parcel of Indians taking the bark from the pines to cover the huts in the Fort; many of the officers were present, noticing how neatly the Indians arranged the bark. Among those present that I recollect, were Gens. Jackson, Gaines and Glasscock; Cols. Breasly and King; Maj. Floyd and Capt. Bee. While we were there, a Georgian by the name of Jabez Gilbert came up. I knew Gilbert; he was pretty well smoked—soap and water would have helped the looks both of himself and clothes. Some eight or ten of these Nashville youngsters seized him, and said they would throw him into the river, which was but a few yards off. One of the young men, I think, was named Ayres, and perhaps a Lieutenant. He step-ped up to Gen. Jackson, and said: "General, we have a notion to wash that fellow." The General said nothing, but hung his head and smiled. That made me mad. They dragged Gilbert nearly to the water's edge. I remarked to Gen. Glasscock, that was one of his men ; I repeated it several times, but Glasscock said nothing. I then spoke out loud, and remarked that he was a Georgian, and had claims on me. I then walked to where Gilbert was, pulled him away from them, and ordered him to go to his quarters. They then attempted to seize me. I tapped, or pushed one of them over ; and another I pushed into the water, where it was about knee deep.

Col. Breasly, who had been, or was looking to be arrested, had made me a present of his side arms, which I had under my hunting shirt, and showed to the boys, and that ended the row at the water.

I walked back, and took my seat not far from where Gen. Jackson and the others were sitting. This man Ayres came up and commenc- en a sort of quarrel with me, and said that Gen. Jackson saw it, and had not interferred, and that it was none of my business ; besides, he said, I had no command among the whites, and that I had better at- tend to my Indians. I told him it mattered not where my command was ; that when I saw such chaps as him out of their place, I would put them in it. I discovered that the General was mad, for I had not been very choice about words or insinuations. He rose to his feet and said he had seen as big men as I was thrown into the water. I remarked to him that he might, but that he had not men enough in his Life Guard to put me in, and if he liked he could try it.

Maj. Twiggs at this time stepped near, and gave me to understand that I had better say no more, and to go to my quarters, and remark- ed to Ayres, at the same time, "Young man, you put out from here." Twiggs and Capt. Bee were the only men that said a word. Capt. Bee turned off, and spoke so as to be heard by those who were listening, and said : "Woodward is right, and the Georgians ought to love him."

As I walked off, Gen. Jackson cursed me for a damned long, Indian looking son-of-a-bitch—(I recollect his language well.) As he made that speech, I turned and said to him, that I had some of the blood, but neither boasted of, nor was ashamed of it. I went to my quarters, and either sent a note or got Capt. Brown to go to the General, (I now forget which,) and say to him that I regretted having incurred his displeasure, and that if he had no further use for my services, I would quit his camp.

That evening or the next morning he sent for me to go to his quarters. He said to me that I done right in preventing the volun- teers from throwing the militiaman in the water, but said I was too self-willed, and did not observe a proper respect towards my superi- ors, and that he wished the matter to drop there, and wished me to remain. There the matter ended.

I could not help laughing to myself at the idea of the difference the old General then made (and which is often made yet) between volunteers and militia, for I had always looked upon volunteers and drafted men both, as being militia, until they had been well trained. Though I believe the word militia signifies a national force or trained band— and all new troops, both volunteers and drafted men, are alike until they are made regulars by training.

From Fort Gadsden we marched to Micasucky, where we had a little brush. There were a few Georgians, some Tennesseeans, under Maj. Russell, a fine fighter, and some friendly Indians in the skirmish— there were but seven Indians killed, but every man along killed one of them. The next was the McIntosh fight, where Mrs. Dill was rescued, which I have given you an accout of before. Col. Butler's account of that is a very incorrect one, as will be recollected by those who were along, and have read his report of that fight. But there is nothing which is more exaggerated generally than the official reports of fights, and particularly those little skirmishes with Indians. The severest brush that I was engaged in during that campaign, was at the Negro Village, near Bowlegs' Town, on the Sawanee. There were only about three hundred friendly Indians, and but four white men engaged in that fight—Isaac Brown, Jack Carter, James Finley, and myself. Col. Williamson, by some means, misunderstood Gen. Jackson's orders, or mistook his place in time of that fight. For if Gen. Jackson's orders had been strictly carried out, and the place of attack strictly observed, very few Indians and negroes could have escaped. But as it turned out, a few Indians had the brunt to bear, as will be recollected by those familiar with that campaign. This fight was in April, but I now forget on what day of the month. The next day I crossed the river with some five hundred Indians, by swimming, and carrying our guns in one hand. We pursued the Indians that day and a part of the next; killed a few Indians, and took a few women and children prisoners, as well as caught a few negroes. On our return to camp, it was in the evening; the man Robert Ambrista happened to get between our lines and the army, and was picked up and made a prisoner, and that ended the Seminole war, so far as I was engaged in it. At the time Ambrista and Cook were picked up at Sawanee, Arbusthnot was a prisoner at St. Marks, which was then in charge of Capt. Vashon. You have heard of the Arbusthnot and Ambrista case. And those who have, or think they have a knowledge of that matter, have made up their minds for and against, long since, and anything that I could say now would do no good. I think it likely, could their lives have been spared, their families at least would have been more benefitted, our country would have sustained no loss, and the consciences of some men, on mature reflection, would have rested easier. And no doubt at the time they were executed, some could have been found of our own people who had been equally guilty, in furnishing the Indians material to do mischief with.

While I was in Florida with the natives from the Chehawtown, some

Georgians under the command of a fool Yankee, by the name of Obed Wright; went to Chehaw, burned and plundered the town, and killed a few old men, some women and children, and among others killed old Howard, who was known as the native chief. The news reached Gen. Jackson while he was at Pensacola. He ordered Maj. Davis, of the ordnance department, to go into Georgia, arrest Wright, and carry him to his (Jackson's) camp, let that be where it might. Maj. Davis arrested Wright, I think, in Louisville. He carried him to Milledgeville where he tried to make his escape. Maj. Davis called on me, as I then had returned home, to aid him in carrying Wright to the army. I not thinking about the impropriety of taking a man by military process, and a private citizen too, out of his State to be tried by a military tribunal, and that, perhaps out of the United States, seized Wright, put him on a horse, and was about being off when Gen. Clark came up, learned what was going on, and said Wright should go no further ; and said he would be one to defend the rights of a citizen against Gen. Jackson and his whole force. Gov. Rabun had a writ of *habeas corpus* issued, and Wright was released. Maj. Davis was highly pleased at gitting rid of his charge. Not long afterwards, I received a letter from the General stating that he was well pleased at my offering my services to Maj. Davis, in aiding to bring that murderer to justice ; and that as I had, on a former occasion, intimated to him that I would like to be in the regular army, if I then wished, he would procure for me a commission. I declined.

That was the end of my services in the United States until 1836, and as there was scarcely a youngster about Columbus, Georgia, or Montgomery, Alabama, who had ever seen Blackstone's Commentaries, or read the Georgia Justice, or Aiken's Digest, or seen a Root Doctor, or read medicine as far as Salts, but was Aid to somebody, or some one else, and among them you will, no doubt, if you wish, get the whole of that affair complete.

After I quit the army in 1818, I went to Washington city with some half-breed Indians. I visited the eastern shore of Maryland, went into Delaware, returned to Georgia, and then went to Alabama and fixed for another settlement. 1 carried a few new negroes and settled them below old Montgomery, in Autauga county. In the spring of 1819, I returned to Georgia to aid Gen. Watson in running the line between Georgia and Florida. I got some Uchee Indians to pack horses and hunt for him, as provision was scarce. After I returned to Milledgeville, I took a trip to Alabama as low as Claiborne. I returned to Georgia, wrote a letter to Gen. Jackson. notifying him of an enterprise that I wished to engage in, (he and I had talked on the subject while in Florida). I have his answer to my letter now, and will send it to you, and you can do what you please with it. It was written on the 30th of September, and mailed at Nashville on the 1st of October, 1819. I was engaged in a little affair in 1813, for a few weeks, but most of those who were along, and myself, differed in our views about patriotism, and I quit.

I see Capt. Cain is dead. He was a man of good heart, and I will let that matter and those that were engaged, rest. Gen. Jackson's letter will explain to you what I was engaged in shortly after I got it. Here I and my crowd differed again about patriotism. In 1820, I returned to Alabama and was married on the 3d of August of that year. The Brigadier General had to be elected by the commissioned officers of the Brigade. The candidates were Col. Joseph H. Howard, Gilbert Shearer, Andrew Taprid, Jonas Brown, William Gray, the man who fought Joe Kemp the first fight for a hundred dollars, and myself. I was elected in August, 1820, and was commissioned on the 13th of September of the same year by Thomas Bibb, who was discharging the duties of Governor, by virtue of his office as President of the Senate of the State.

I remained in Alabama some twenty years; managed my pecuniary matters badly most of the time; was very poor; was sold out twice by the sheriff; always voted on the weak side; was not very popular; often spoke too quick and too freely; had a family that was interesting to me at least, consequently had often to submit to indignities or insults from a little short stock that under other circumstances I should have slapped a rod. In 1841, I moved to Arkansas, and lived there twelve years. The climate proved fatal to all of my family except my eldest son, and it has so preyed upon him and myself that we are nothing more than the wrecks of what once were men.

Now, sir, these sketches have been written in a poor style, but have been faithfully narrated; and perhaps you may be able to glean from them, in an imperfect manner, a part of the information you desired. and whether you find them interesting or not, from the rapid manner in which my health has declined of late, I think it probable they are the last I shall give you or any one else. I shall close this by giving you what I think was the true disposition and character of Gen. Jackson.

If he was not the most sensible and best man that I have known, he was the greatest man, with a large portion of the American people, whom I have had any thing to do with. His mind was stronger and better cultivated than many have thought it to be; a man of bitter prejudices and unforgiving disposition, and a true friend when he really proposed it. He could not be corrupted with money, strictly honest in all monied transactions, despised flattery, though he often had it heaped upon him by the quantity, in his latter days. The only ones who could flatter him were those whom he looked upon as being so low they could have no motive, and those who stood so high as not to be suspected. He preferred having his own judgment respected more than that of the balance of the world. If he bet ten dollars on a horse race, he would pay a hundred rather than lose the ten; for with the loss of the ten dollars would go his judgment. He would never, for a moment, suffer himself to think that those he placed in office would act dishonest—he being honest in money matters himself —and that was the cause of there being some defaulters in office during his administration. He would admit of no superior, and was jealous of those whom the people looked upon as his equals, and was not at all times a judge of his true friends. There were thousands who appreciated him properly and admired him for his good qualities, but opposed some of his arbitrary measures, and some had not voted for him. These he looked upon as his enemies, and never missed an opportunity to deal them a blow under the fifth rib. His popularity, at one time, and for a long time, was almost irresistible. He would suffer it used in the support of a friend, regardless of every thing, when silence on his part would have placed him in a more enviable attitude with the more reflecting and intelligent portion of mankind. I will cite one instance among many to show how far he would go. It has been the custom, and is expected, that demagogues and politicians will use every means to carry their points in elections. But there has always been one rule observed among our army and naval officers, and it never should be violated; for they established the rule and take them according to number, they are and have been the most thorough gentlemen I have any knowledge of. That rule was never for one officer to speak disparagingly of another, unless it was well known that he had been guilty of a gross violation of duty, or something else, that had rendered him an unfit associate for the balance. Gen. Harrison had been a Major General in the army and resigned. Gen. Jackson succeeded to the command which Gen. Harrison would have held had he continued in the service. Gen. Jackson did much. He achieved a victory that the history of wars seldom records. The American people thanked him, they rewarded him, placed him in the highest office known to civilized men. But not to their credit do I say they submitted to his iron will, and in some instances a gross violation of their rights. It is well known, in a country like ours, that in some instances too high an estimate has been placed on military fame. It has governed in some of the most important elections, and has resulted in but little good to the country. In 1840, Gen. Harrison was a candidate for the Presidency. His friends seized upon his military deeds, and other things, as had Gen. Jackson's friends done before. Instead of remaining quiet and letting the people arrange their own matters, Gen. Jackson departed so far from what I think should have been his proper course as to write a letter, giving the people, and particularly his own friends, to understand that he never had looked upon Gen. Harrison as a military man. This was objectionable, coming from the source it did. The times and circumstances at the time, some men have lived, have had much to do in building up or pulling down their fortunes. It is quite likely that if Oliver

Cromwell had lived in England at any other time than that in which
he did live, from the reign of Egbert down to Victoria he would have
been looked upon as being what he really was—a base hypocrite.—
Clay, Webster, Calhoun and Gaston, (if the latter had possessed more
ambition) would have been great at any age of the world, and so
would Gen. Jackson have been more than an ordinary man at any time.
And had he been old enough, and placed at the head of any army in
the revolution, no doubt he would have distinguished himself, but
never would have been rated higher than many engaged in that service, and perhaps not as high as Green, Wayne, Stark, Daniel Morgan,
or Ethan Allen. And had' there, by chance or otherwise, been any
one who was placed higher in the scale of greatness than himself, I
think it quite likely that he would have evinced, or have shown, to
some extent, a kind of jealousy to Charles Lee or Horatio Gates.
Those of the Revolution were a different people to most of those in
Gen. Jackson's time. In the Revolution, men were willing to serve,
and if by chance they were killed, it would answer for their friends to
read and speak of their deeds of daring. But not so in Gen. Jackson's
time. There were too many who chose to live and see their names
puffed in the newspapers, whether they merited it or not. Gen. Jackson knew the people he lived amongst, and knew how to control them
and did do it.

The best evidence I can give of his being a great man is, that without money and friends he raised himself from an obscure Irish boy to
the head of this nation, and was the most popular man that ever was
and perhaps ever will be in it again. I have not said Irish boy from
any invidious motive, or to detract any thing from his true merit.—
For I think if his true origin were known, it would only add to his
standing, and prove to the world that he descended from a race of
the right blood to make great men. One thing can be said of a truth,
that he made more little would-be great-men, the last twenty years of
his life, than God has made truly great ones for the last two centuries.
And if his ambition, at times, caused him to err, his love of country
made him a good patriot; and the American people will cherish his
memory, particularly those living in his time, while he sleeps quietly
where the laudations of sycophantic and hypocritical friends and the
reproaches of his enemies cannot interrupt his repose.

Yours, truly,

T. S. WOODWARD.

WHEELING, WINN PARISH, LOUISIANA, }
December 25th, 1858. }

J. J. HOOPER, ESQ.,

Dear Sir: This is Christmas—a day in early life that I waited with
impatience for its appearance ; but it now seems to come and go so
fast that it differs little from any other day with me, as all come in

such quick succession as to admonish me that, live as long as I may, that I am to witness the return of but few more Christmases. But as I am alone, and have recovered a little strength after being reduced quite low from a fit of severe hemorrhage from the stomach, as well as a slight one from the lungs, I have concluded to write a little. I see in your paper of the 17th inst., that some of my letters will make their appearance, in pamphlet form, in the course of a few weeks. I sent you a package a few days back, containing many little sketches of my early life. I was very sick when I wrote them, and in them you will no doubt find the same weakness in me, that is too often discovered in most old people. No matter what they write or talk about, whether interesting to others or not, they are always better posted in things that pertained to them in early life, and often let the world know more of family matters than a proper prudence might authorize. And should this happen to be my case, in the sketches sent you the other day, all that I can say now is, that they are truths which some might think had better been let alone. And as you desired some time back to know of me something of the Government service I had been in, and the little fights that I had witnessed—and as I went so far as to bring in the Florida War of 1817 and 1818—and for fear you may think I wish to claim some credit for being along, and would willingly impose upon you and your readers, what has been imposed upon the world, I must here go into a little detail of that Seminole or Florida Campaign, or at least give you a correct list of the killed in the expedition, and who by. I shall give you facts— and he that contradicts 'them, knows nothing of the expedition, or wilfully lies.

I mentioned to you that in Glasscock's first expedition, in 1817, some Hitcheta or Seminole Indians, under the control of a Chief known as Chenubba, killed Tom Lee, and cut off his head—killed Sam Loftis, and scalped him. I will now give you a correct list of the number of whites killed, and the number of Indians killed by the whites in Gen. Jackson's march to Sawany, where the Seminole campaign proper, ended. I crossed Flint River in 1818, in March, with a party of friendly Indians—the day of the month not recollected. The second day, we fell in with a few Indians—killed two and captured one; that one we carried to Gen. Jackson's camp, and while fixing for camping at night, the prisoner attempted to make his escape. A portion of Twiggs' command was on guard, shot and killed him. That was the first Indian killed by the whites. The next night we camped on a bluff on the Apalachicola River. A white man, blinded by the fire-light or something else, walked over the bluff into the river, and was drowned. At Mickasucky we had a skirmish with the Indians—in which some friendly Indians, a few Georgians, and some Tennesseeans under Maj. Russell, were engaged. A man named Majors Henderson killed one Indian, (for which he served in the Legislature as long as he pleased.) 'He shot him in the back while the Indian was trying to shoot at Billy Mitchell and myself—this I saw. There were five other hostile Indians killed in the fight; the friendly Indians claimed the killing of them—so did the whites. There happened to be an old Uchee Indian, known as old Joe, who said he was only on a visit to Mickasucky, who did not run off with the rest; he was made a prisoner. After the little skirmish was over, a young man from Tennessee, named Tucker, saw the crowd around Joe; Tucker rode up, and asked if that was a hostile Indian—sone one answered "yes." He drew a horseman's pistol from his holster, fired at Joe and missed him. Joe had a British musket across his lap, which had not been taken from him; he raised the musket, fired at Tucker, who was on his horse; the ball entered between the tip of his chin and his throat, and passed out at the top of his head, killing him instantly. The Indians killed Joe upon the spot; so there were seven Indians and one white man killed in that fight. Joe's head was as white as heads generally get to be. His musket fell into the hands of Maj. Nix, of the army. He gave it to me. I loaned it to Capt. Abram Bourland, late of Lowndes county, Alabama, in 1819, to carry a runaway negro to Alabama; he loaned it to Mr. Caleb Niblet, to fire-hunt with; and it was the gun that Niblet, and Billy Boswell, of Cahaba, killed Mall's cattle and Ned Covington's mare and colt with, which many of the old settlers well recollect. So ends the Mickasucky fight.

At St. Marks, Arburthnot was arrested, and afterwards hanged. At the McIntosh fight, Isaac Brown killed one Indian. On our march from St. Marks to Sawany, the old half-breed, Blount, and I were ahead, and discovered some Indians that were cutting a bee tree. We halted for the purpose of getting some friendly Indians to surround them, but some of the Tennessee mounted men came up, and we pointed them out and requested the mounted men to wait until the friendly Indians could come up—that it was possible the bee-hunters might be friendly Indians; but they made a rush upon the Indians, who proved to be three men, a woman and two children; they made no resistance, but the mounted men killed one of the men, broke another's thigh, shot the woman through the body, shot off the under jaw of one of the children, and broke an arm of the other—the third man made his escape. On my return by the place, the woman and one child were lying dead—the child with the broken arm, and the one with his thigh broke, had left. The next white man that was killed, was a man sitting in a crowd where another white man was picking his gun flint; the gun went off and killed him. That was the day we reached Sawanee. While at that place, we picked up Robert Ambrista, commonly known as Ambrister; he was afterward3 shot, having been tried and condemned as a spy—which affair you know all about.

. You have now the whole of what was done in the Seminole cam-

paign of 1817–'18, except what was done by the friendly Indians. I
think Mr. Grantland, of Milledgeville, could furnish you with the official report of the McIntosh fight—it was in April, 1818, and was
published in a Milledgeville paper, either by Grantland or Hines.
The number killed at Sawanee by the friendly Indians, I do not know,
as a part of them were killed in the river. There were but four white
men with the Indians or in the fight at Sawanee, who were Brown,
Finley, Carter and myself; and unless a stray shot from one of our
guns killed an Indian or a negro, the friendly Indians are entitled to
all the credit of that affair. I was not at the taking of Pensacola, and
can not tell what was done there. Now, if the firing of a few guns,
and occasionally killing an Indian or two, can be considered fights, I
have seen many. But as I did not think proper to detail them at a
time, when perhaps a little capital might have been made of them, I
will dispense with it now.

While I am at this, let me correct a few more errors that many have
fallen into. You no doubt, as many others, have seen the official reports of various Indian fights, where the whites whipped the Indians
and no dead ones left on the ground, but great signs of the killed and
wounded being dragged off. All that is necessary to explain this
matter, is to ask you how many men it would take to carry off a dead
man faster than a slow footman could follow? I have seen much
Indian skirmishing in my time, (and those that know me best believe
I state facts,) but never have I seen the first Indian, either friendly or
hostile, run the least risk to carry off a dead friend. I have seen
them aid wounded ones, and that's all. Indians know the value of a
dead Indian, about as well as whites. And it was once the custom
among them, if one was killed, and marked with a knife, his mother
would not bury him. To speak the honest truth, they never have
been killed; and, in fact, there have not been as many warriors in
the Creek and Seminole Nations, in my time, as have been supposed
by some to have been killed in the little wars among those people,
from 1812 to 1836, and down to the removal of Billy Bowlegs West.
History is a thing often exaggerated, and by none so much so as the
official reports of those little Indian fights.

* * * * * * * * * * * *

In a package I sent you some time back, giving you the names of
Agents, Indians and others, I mentioned Ogillis Ineah or Menauway,
the Chief that commanded at Horse-Shoe. He was the Chief that
headed the party that killed McIntosh, Sam Hawkins, and others. I
knew him well, and he knew me, and knew that I disliked his killing
McIntosh. At a Council at Sechalitchar,* in 1835, he got very angry
with Hopoithleyoholo and let the secret out about the McIntosh affair.
He looked at me and Capt. Walker, held up his hands, and said,
"Here are the hands that are stained with the blood of McIntosh, and
I am now ready to stain them again in the blood of his enemies, and
those who made me the dupe of their foul designs. When I done the
deed I thought I was right, but I am sorry." I will give you more of
him at some other time. I know the whole of that affair, but the
actors in it are mostly gone to rest, So let them sleep on, as it can
do no good to bring it up.   Yours truly,
                                        T. S. WOODWARD.

* This name is a puzzling one in the MS. I hope I have given it correctly, but am
by no means certain.   H.

Made in the USA
Columbia, SC
29 November 2024

47880937R00096